The Cold War: A Very Short Introduction

'McMahon has produced a commanding short narrative of a vital period in recent world history. Clear, concise, and compelling, *The Cold War* is a superb primer on the subject.'
Fredrik Logevall, University of California, Santa Barbara

VERY SHORT INTRODUCTIONS are for anyone wanting a stimulating and accessible way into a new subject. They are written by experts, and have been translated into more than 45 different languages.

The series began in 1995, and now covers a wide variety of topics in every discipline. The VSI library now contains over 500 volumes—a Very Short Introduction to everything from Psychology and Philosophy of Science to American History and Relativity—and continues to grow in every subject area.

Titles in the series include the following:

Robert McMahon

THE COLD WAR

A Very Short Introduction

OXFORD
UNIVERSITY PRESS

OXFORD
UNIVERSITY PRESS

Great Clarendon Street, Oxford OX2 6DP

Oxford University Press is a department of the University of Oxford.
It furthers the University's objective of excellence in research, scholarship,
and education by publishing worldwide in

Oxford New York

Auckland Bangkok Buenos Aires Cape Town Chennai
Dar es Salaam Delhi Hong Kong Istanbul Karachi Kolkata
Kuala Lumpur Madrid Melbourne Mexico City Mumbai Nairobi
São Paulo Shanghai Taipei Tokyo Toronto

Oxford is a registered trade mark of Oxford University Press
in the UK and in certain other countries

Published in the United States
by Oxford University Press Inc., New York

© Robert McMahon 2003

The moral rights of the author have been asserted

Database right Oxford University Press (maker)

First published as a Very Short Introduction 2003

British Library Cataloguing in Publication Data

Data available

Library of Congress Cataloging in Publication Data

Data available

ISBN 978-0-19-280178-4

28

Typeset by RefineCatch Ltd, Bungay, Suffolk
Printed in Great Britain by
Ashford Colour Press Ltd, Gosport,Hants.

Contents

Preface to this edition

Writing a compact history of the conflict that dominated and largely defined international affairs for nearly half a century has proven an assignment at once challenging, exciting, and daunting. Detailed monographs, many of them excellent and most considerably longer than the present volume, exist for virtually every one of the major events, crises, trends, and personalities discussed in this necessarily slim book. Vigorous, oft-times vituperative scholarly debates, moreover, have raged over almost every aspect of the Cold War's history. Those debates have been enlivened, and deepened, in recent years with the release of previously secret documentary evidence from archives in the United States, Russia, Eastern Europe, China, and elsewhere – and by the fresh perspectives afforded by the passage of time. This book, consequently, does not – nor could it – purport to be the last word on the Cold War or to represent anything approaching a comprehensive history of that complex, multi-faceted conflict.

Rather, in keeping with the general objectives of the *Very Short Introduction* series, my goal has been to provide a broad, interpretive overview, one accessible to students and general readers alike. This book offers a general account of the Cold War, spanning the period from 1945 to the final denouement of the Soviet-American confrontation in 1990. It elucidates key events, trends, and themes, drawing in so doing from some of the most important recent scholarship on the Cold War. I have sought, above all, to provide readers with an essential foundation for understanding and assessing one of the seminal events in modern world history.

Inevitably, I have had to make difficult choices in terms of what to cover, and what to omit, about a conflict that spanned four and a half decades and encompassed virtually the entire globe. Limitations of space precluded treatment of some significant episodes and compelled the most abbreviated possible treatment of others. I also decided to pay short shrift to the military dimensions of the Cold War, partly because other volumes in this series will be devoted to the Korean and the Vietnam wars. What follows, then, is a 'very short introduction' to the Cold War, as the title promises, written from an international perspective and from a post-Cold War angle of vision. Key guiding questions addressed by the narrative include: How, when, and why did the Cold War begin?; Why did it last so long?; Why did it move from its initial origins in postwar Europe to embrace almost the entire world?; Why did it end so suddenly and unexpectedly?; And what impact did it have?

I am grateful to Robert Zieger, Lawrence Freedman, and Melvyn Leffler, each of whom read the manuscript and offered valuable suggestions for its improvement. I also thank Rebecca O'Connor for encouragement, advice, and support throughout, along with the entire Oxford University Press editorial staff, who made working on this book a pleasure.

List of illustrations

The publisher and the author apologize for any errors or omissions in the above list. If contacted they will be pleased to rectify these at the earliest opportunity.

List of maps

Chapter 1
World War II and the destruction of the old order

Explanations for the onset of the Cold War must begin with World War II. A conflict that ranks, by any conceivable measure, as the most destructive in human history, World War II brought unparalleled levels of death, devastation, privation, and disorder.

'The conflagration of 1939–1945 was so wrenching, so total, so profound, that a world was overturned,' notes historian Thomas G. Paterson, 'not simply a human world of healthy and productive laborers, farmers, merchants, financiers, and intellectuals, not simply a secure world of close-knit families and communities, not simply a military world of Nazi storm troopers and Japanese kamikazes, but all that and more.' By unhinging as well 'the world of stable politics, inherited wisdom, traditions, institutions, alliances, loyalties, commerce and classes', the war created the conditions that made great power conflict highly likely, if not inevitable.

A world overturned

Approximately 60 million people lost their lives as a direct result of the war, fully two-thirds of them noncombatants. The war's losers, the Axis states of Germany, Japan, and Italy, suffered more than 3 million civilian deaths; their conquerors, the Allies, suffered far more: at least 35 million civilian deaths. An astonishing 10 to 20%

of the total populations of the Soviet Union, Poland, and Yugoslavia perished, between 4 and 6% of the total populations of Germany, Italy, Austria, Hungary, Japan, and China. If the exact toll of this wrenching global conflagration continues to defy all efforts at statistical precision, the magnitude of the human losses it claimed surely remains as shockingly unfathomable two generations after World War II as it was in the conflict's immediate aftermath.

At war's end, much of the European continent lay in ruins. British Prime Minister Winston S. Churchill, in characteristically vivid prose, described postwar Europe as 'a rubble heap, a charnel house, a breeding ground of pestilence and hate'. Berlin was 'an utter wasteland', observed correspondent William Shirer, 'I don't think there has ever been such destruction on such a scale'. In fact, many of the largest cities of central and eastern Europe suffered comparable levels of devastation; 90% of the buildings in Cologne, Düsseldorf, and Hamburg were gutted by Allied bombing, 70% of those in the centre of Vienna. In Warsaw, reported John Hershey, the Germans had 'destroyed, systematically, street by street, alley by alley, house by house. Nothing is left except a mockery of architecture'. US Ambassador Arthur Bliss Lane, upon entering that war-ravaged city in July 1945, wrote: 'The sickening sweet odor of burned human flesh was a grim warning that we were entering a city of the dead.' In France, fully one-fifth of the nation's buildings were damaged or destroyed; in Greece, one-quarter. Even never-occupied Great Britain suffered extensive damage, principally from Nazi bombing, while losing an estimated one-quarter of its total national wealth in the course of the conflict. Soviet losses were the most severe of all: at least 25 million dead, another 25 million rendered homeless, 6 million buildings destroyed, and much of the country's industrial plant and productive farmland laid to waste. Across Europe, an estimated 50 million of the war's survivors had been uprooted by the war, some 16 million of them euphemistically termed 'displaced persons' by the victorious Allies.

Conditions in postwar Asia were nearly as grim. Almost all of Japan's cities had been ravaged by relentless US bombing, with 40% of its urban areas completely destroyed. Tokyo, Japan's largest metropolis, was gutted by Allied firebombing that levelled more than half of its buildings. Hiroshima and Nagasaki met an even more dire fate as the twin atomic blasts that brought the Pacific War to a close left them obliterated. Approximately 9 million Japanese were homeless when their leaders finally surrendered. In China, a battleground for more than a decade, the industrial plant of Manchuria lay in shambles, the rich farmland of the Yellow River engulfed in floods. As many as 4 million Indonesians perished as a direct or indirect result of the conflict. One million Indians succumbed to war-induced famine in 1943, another million people in Indo-China two years later. Although much of Southeast Asia was spared the direct horrors of war visited upon Japan, China, and various Pacific islands, other parts, such as the Philippines and Burma, were not so fortunate. During the war's final stage, 80% of Manila's buildings were razed in savage fighting. Equally brutal combat in Burma, in the testimony of wartime leader Ba Maw, 'had reduced an enormous part of the country to ruins'.

The vast swath of death and destruction precipitated by the war left not only much of Europe and Asia in ruins but the old international order as well. 'The whole world structure and order that we had inherited from the nineteenth century was gone', marvelled US Assistant Secretary of State Dean Acheson. Indeed, the Eurocentric international system that had dominated world affairs for the past 500 years had, virtually overnight, vanished. Two continent-sized military behemoths – already being dubbed superpowers – had risen in its stead, each intent upon forging a new order consonant with its particular needs and values. As the war moved into its final phase, even the most casual observer of world politics could see that the United States and the Soviet Union held most of the military, economic, and diplomatic cards. On one basic goal, those

3

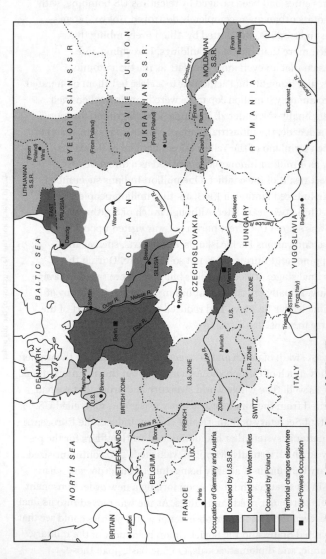

Map 1. Central Europe after World War II.

adversaries-turned-allies were in essential accord: that some semblance of authority and stability needed to be restored with dispatch – and not just to those areas directly affected by the war but to the broader international system as well. The task was as urgent as it was daunting since, as Under Secretary of State Joseph Grew warned in June 1945: 'Anarchy may result from the present economic distress and political unrest.'

The immediate roots of the Cold War, at least in broad, structural terms, lay in the intersection between a world rendered prostrate by a devastating global conflict and the conflicting recipes for international order that Washington and Moscow sought to impose on that pliable, war-shattered world. Some degree of conflict invariably results whenever a prevailing international order and its accompanying balance of power system are overturned. One would certainly expect no less when the overturning occurs with such shattering suddenness. The tension, suspicion, and rivalry that came to plague US–Soviet relations in the immediate aftermath of war was, in that elemental sense, hardly a surprise. Yet the *degree* and *scope* of the ensuing conflict, and particularly its *duration*, cannot be explained by appeals to structural forces alone. History, after all, offers numerous examples of great powers following the path of compromise and cooperation, opting to act in concert so as to establish a mutually acceptable international order capable of satisfying the most fundamental interests of each. Scholars have employed the term 'great power condominium' to describe such systems. Despite the hopes of some leading officials in both the United States and the Soviet Union, however, that would not be the case this time. The reasons why go to the heart of the question of Cold War origins. In brief, it was the divergent aspirations, needs, histories, governing institutions, and ideologies of the United States and the Soviet Union that turned unavoidable tensions into the epic four-decade confrontation that we call the Cold War.

American visions of postwar order

The United States emerged from the wreckage of World War II with relatively moderate losses. Although some 400,000 of the nation's soldiers and sailors gave their lives in the struggle against the Axis powers, approximately three-quarters of them on the battlefield, it bears emphasizing that those numbers represent less than 1% of the war's overall death toll and less than 2% of the losses suffered by America's Soviet partner. For most US civilians, in stunning contrast to their counterparts across Europe, East Asia, North Africa, and elsewhere, the war meant not suffering and privation but prosperity – even abundance. The nation's gross domestic product doubled between 1941 and 1945, bestowing the wonders of a highly productive, full-employment economy on a citizenry that had become accustomed to the deprivations imposed by a decade-long depression. Real wages rose rapidly and dramatically during the war years, and homefront Americans found themselves awash in a cornucopia of now-affordable consumer goods. 'The American people', remarked the director of the Office of War Mobilization and Reconversion, 'are in the pleasant predicament of having to learn to live 50 percent better than they have ever lived before.'

In March 1945, newly installed President Harry S. Truman was merely stating the self-evident when he commented: 'We have emerged from this war the most powerful nation in the world – the most powerful nation, perhaps, in all history.' Yet neither the economic benefits conferred on the American people by the war nor the soaring military power, productive strength, and international prestige attained by their nation during the struggle against Axis aggression could lessen the frightening uncertainties of the new world ushered in by the war. The Japanese attack at Pearl Harbor decisively shattered the illusion of invulnerability that Americans had enjoyed ever since the end of the Napoleonic Wars of the early 19th century. The obsession with national security that became so central a motif of US foreign and defence policy throughout the Cold War era can be traced back directly to the myth-puncturing events that culminated with the Japanese strike of 7 December 1941. Not until the terrorist attacks on New York and Washington 60 years later would Americans again experience so direct, and so wholly unanticipated, an assault on their homeland.

Military strategists took several lessons from the bold Japanese strike, each of which carried profound implications for the future. They became convinced, first, that technology, and especially air power, had so contracted the globe that America's vaunted two-ocean barrier no longer afforded sufficient protection from external assault. True security now required a defence that began well beyond the home shores – a defence in depth, in military parlance. That concept led defence officials of the Roosevelt and Truman administrations to advocate the establishment of an integrated, global network of US-controlled air and naval bases, as well as the negotiation of widespread military air transit rights. Together, those would allow the United States to project its power more easily into potential trouble spots and to stifle or deter prospective enemies long before they gained the power to strike at American territory. A sense of how extensive US military base requirements were can be gleaned from a 1946 list of 'essential' sites compiled by the State Department; it included, among other locales, Burma, Canada, the Fiji Islands, New Zealand, Cuba, Greenland, Ecuador, French Morocco, Senegal, Iceland, Liberia, Panama, Peru, and the Azores.

Second, and even more broadly, senior American strategists determined that the nation's military power must never again be allowed to atrophy. US military strength, they were agreed, must form a core element of the new world order. The Franklin D. Roosevelt and Harry S. Truman administrations were, accordingly, insistent upon maintaining naval and air forces second to none; a strong military presence in the Pacific; dominance of the Western hemisphere; a central role in the occupations of defeated adversaries Italy, Germany, Austria, and Japan; and a continued monopoly on the atomic bomb. Even before the eruption of the Cold War, US strategic planners were operating from an extraordinarily expansive concept of national security.

That broad vision of the nation's security requirements was reinforced by a third, overarching lesson that US policy-makers drew from the World War II experience: namely, that never again could a hostile state, or coalition of states, be allowed to gain preponderant control over the populations, territories, and resources of Europe and East Asia. The Eurasian heartland, as geopoliticians were fond of labelling it, ranked as the world's greatest strategic-economic prize; its combination of rich natural resources, advanced industrial infrastructure, skilled labour, and sophisticated military facilities made it the fulcrum of world power, as the events of 1940–1 made painfully clear. When the Axis powers seized control over much of Eurasia in the early 1940s, they gained the wherewithal to wage protracted war, subvert the world economy, commit heinous crimes against humanity, and threaten and ultimately attack the Western hemisphere. If such an eventuality came to pass again, US defence officials worried, the international system would once again be badly destabilized, the balance of world power dangerously distorted, and the physical safety of the United States put at grave risk. Moreover, even if a direct attack on the United States could be averted, American leaders would still be forced to prepare for one – and that would mean a radical increase in both military spending and the size of its permanent defence establishment, a reconfiguration of the domestic economy, and the curtailment of cherished economic and political freedoms at home. Axis dominance of Eurasia, in short, or control over Eurasia by any future enemy, would thus also jeopardize the political economy of freedom so crucial to core US beliefs and values. The World War II experience thus offered hard lessons about the critical importance of maintaining a favourable balance of power in Eurasia.

The military-strategic dimensions of world order were, in American thinking, inseparable from the economic dimensions. US planners viewed the establishment of a freer and more open international economic system as equally indispensable to the new order they were determined to construct from the ashes of history's most horrific conflict. Experience had instructed them, Secretary of State Cordell Hull recalled, that free trade stood as an essential prerequisite for peace. The autarky, closed trading blocs, and nationalistic barriers to foreign investment and currency convertibility that had characterized the depression decade just encouraged interstate rivalry and conflict. A more open world, according to the American formula, would be a more prosperous world; and a more prosperous world would, in turn, be a more stable and peaceful world. To achieve those ends, the United States pushed hard in wartime diplomatic councils for a multilateral economic regime of liberalized trade, equal investment opportunities for all nations, stable exchange rates, and full currency convertibility. At the Bretton Woods Conference late in 1944, the United States gained general acceptance of those principles, along with support for the establishment of two key supranational bodies, the International Monetary Fund and the International Bank for Reconstruction and Development (World Bank), charged with helping to stabilize the global economy. That the United States, the world's leading capitalist state and one that was producing an astonishing 50% of the world's goods and services at war's end, would surely benefit from the new, multilateral commercial regime so vigorously endorsed by the Roosevelt and Truman administrations and the US business community was a given. American ideals here were inextricably interwoven with American interests.

In a December 1944 editorial, the *Chicago Tribune* captured the buoyancy and self-confidence of American society when it proudly proclaimed that it was 'the good fortune of the world', and not just the United States, that 'power and unquestionable intentions' now 'went together' in the Great American Republic. Such convictions about the righteous destiny of the United States tapped deep roots within American history and culture. Elites and non-elites alike accepted the notion that it was their country's historic responsibility to bring about a new, more peaceful, prosperous, and stable world. US leaders betrayed few doubts about the ability of their nation to effect so momentous a transition; nor did they acknowledge any potential conflict between the global order they sought to forge and the needs and interests of the rest of humanity. With the hubris of a people who had known few failures, Americans thought that they could, in Dean Acheson's choice words, 'grab hold of history and make it conform'. Only one significant obstacle loomed. The Soviet Union, cautioned *Life* magazine in July 1945, 'is the number one problem for Americans because it is the only country in the world with the dynamic power to challenge our own conceptions of truth, justice, and the good life'.

Soviet visions of postwar order

The Soviet blueprint for postwar order was also born of deep-rooted security fears. As in the American case, those fears were refracted through the filters of history, culture, and ideology. Soviet memories of Hitler's surprise attack of June 1941 were just as vivid – and far more terrifying – than were American memories of Pearl Harbor. It could hardly have been otherwise in a land that had endured such staggering losses. Of the 15 Soviet Republics, 9 had been occupied in whole or in part by the Germans. Hardly any Soviet citizens remained untouched personally by what they came to sanctify as The Great Patriotic War. Nearly every family lost a loved one; most sacrificed several. In addition to the millions of human lives cut short by the conflict, 1,700 cities and towns, more than 70,000 villages and hamlets, and 31,000 factories were demolished. Leningrad, the country's most historic city, was decimated in a prolonged siege that alone claimed over a million lives. The German invasion also wreaked havoc with the nation's agricultural base, destroying millions of acres of crops and resulting in the slaughter of tens of millions of cattle, hogs, sheep, goats, and horses.

Searing memories of the German attack and occupation merged with other, longer memories – of the German invasion during World War I, of Allied intervention during the Russian civil war, of Napoleon's attempted conquest of Russia at the beginning of the previous century – to induce in the Soviet leadership a veritable obsession with ensuring the protection of their homeland from future territorial violations. The geographical expanse of the Soviet Union, a nation that covered one-sixth of the earth's land mass and was three times larger than the United States, made the challenge of an adequate national defence especially acute. Its two most economically vital regions, European Russia and Siberia, lay at the country's extremes; and each had in the recent past shown itself highly vulnerable to attack. The former fronted on the infamous Polish corridor, the invasion route through which the troops of Napoleon, the Kaiser, and Hitler had so easily poured in the past. The latter had twice within the last 25 years fallen prey to Japanese aggression; Siberia, moreover, shared a vast land border with China, an unstable neighbour still in the throes of revolutionary upheaval. No friendly neighbours, such as Mexico and Canada, and no two-ocean barriers existed to ease the task of Soviet defence planners.

The overwhelming need to defend the Soviet homeland lay at the heart of all Kremlin designs for the postwar world. Blocking the Polish invasion route, or 'gateway', ranked foremost in that regard. Poland, stressed Stalin, was 'a matter of life or death' to his country. 'In the course of twenty-five years the Germans had twice invaded Russia via Poland', Soviet ruler Joseph Stalin lectured US envoy Harry Hopkins in May 1945. 'Neither the British nor the American people had experienced such German invasions which were a horrible thing to endure. . . . It is therefore in Russia's vital interest that Poland should be strong and friendly.' Convinced that the Germans would recover quickly and once again pose a threat to the Soviet Union, Stalin considered it mandatory that steps be taken while the world was still malleable to ensure future Soviet security needs. Those required, at a minimum, that acquiescent, pro-Soviet

11

governments be installed in Poland and other key Eastern European states; that Soviet borders be expanded to their fullest pre-revolutionary extent – meaning the permanent annexation of the Baltic states and the eastern part of pre-war Poland; and that Germany be hobbled through a harsh occupation regime, systematic de-industrialization, and extensive reparations obligations. German reparations could also contribute to the massive rebuilding effort facing the Soviet Union as it sought to recover from the ravages of the war.

Yet those plans, based as they were on the age-old formula of security-through-expansion, needed to be balanced against a countervailing desire to maintain the framework of cooperation with the United States and Great Britain that had evolved, however imperfectly, during the war years. The Kremlin's interest in sustaining the Grand Alliance partnership forged in the heat of total war rested not on sentiment, which had no place in Soviet diplomacy, but on a set of quite practical considerations. First, Soviet rulers recognized that an open break with the West needed to be avoided, at least for the foreseeable future. Given the crippling losses to manpower, resources, and industrial plant inflicted on their nation by the war, a premature conflict with the United States and Great Britain would place the Soviets at a severe disadvantage, a disadvantage made even more palpable after the US demonstration of its atomic capabilities in August 1945. Second, Stalin and his chief lieutenants were hopeful that the United States could be induced to make good on its promise of generous financial support to their reconstruction efforts. A policy of unbridled territorial expansion would likely prove counterproductive, since it could precipitate the very dissolution of the wartime alliance and consequent withholding of economic assistance that they sought to prevent.

Finally, the Soviets were looking to be treated as a respected, responsible great power after being shunned as a pariah state for so long. They craved respect, somewhat paradoxically, from the same capitalist states their ideological convictions taught them to loathe. The Russians wanted not just respect, of course; they insisted upon an equal voice in international councils and acceptance of the legitimacy of their interests. Even more to the point, they sought formal Western recognition of their expanded borders and acceptance of, or at least acquiescence in, their emerging sphere of influence in Eastern Europe. All those considerations served as brakes on any imprudent inclinations to gobble up as much territory as the Red Army's naked power might allow.

The fact that one of history's most brutal, ruthless, and suspicious rulers presided over the Soviet Union's delicate balancing act at this critical juncture adds an unavoidable personal element to the story of Moscow's postwar ambitions. The imperious Stalin completely dominated Soviet policy-making before, during, and after the war, brooking no dissent. In the recollection of Nikita Khrushchev, Stalin's eventual successor, 'he spoke and we listened'. The former Bolshevik revolutionary 'transformed the government he ran and even the country he ruled, during the 1930s, into a gargantuan extension of his own pathologically suspicious personality', suggests historian John Lewis Gaddis. It was a 'supreme act of egoism' that 'spawned innumerable tragedies'. In the aftermath of World War II, Stalin viewed his Western allies, as he viewed all potential

Joseph Stalin

Slight of stature and possessing little by way of charisma or oratorical talent, the Georgian-born Stalin ruled his country with an iron fist from the mid-1920s until his death in 1953. The Soviet dictator tightened his grip on the reins of power during the 1930s – at a frightful price to his own people. As many as 20 million Soviet citizens died as a direct or indirect result of Stalin's forced collectivization of Soviet agriculture and systematic repression.

competitors at home and abroad, with the deepest suspicion and mistrust.

Yet Russian foreign policy cannot be understood as the product, pure and simple, of Stalin's brutishness and unquenchable thirst for dominance, as important as those surely were. For all his ruthlessness and paranoia, and for all his cruelty towards his own people, Stalin pursued a generally cautious, circumspect foreign policy, seeking always to balance opportunity with risk. The Russian dictator invariably calculated with great care the prevailing 'correlation of forces'. He evinced a realist's respect for the superior military and industrial power possessed by the United States and oft-times sought the proverbial half a loaf when pursuit of a full loaf seemed likely to generate resistance. The needs of the Soviet state, which always took precedence for Stalin over the desire to spread communism, dictated a policy that mixed opportunism with caution and an inclination to compromise, not a strategy of aggressive expansion.

The ideology of Marxism-Leninism that undergirded the Soviet state also influenced the outlook and policies of Stalin and his top associates, though in complex, hard-to-pin-down ways. A deep-seated belief in the teachings of Marx and Lenin imparted to them a messianic faith in the future, a reassuring sense of confidence that, whatever travails Moscow might face in the short run, history lay on their side. Stalin and the Kremlin elite assumed conflict between the socialist and capitalist worlds to be inevitable, and they were certain that the forces of proletarian revolution would eventually prevail. They were thus unwilling to press too hard when the correlation of forces seemed so favourable to the West. 'Our ideology stands for offensive operations when possible', as Foreign Minister V. M. Molotov put it, 'and if not we wait'. If ideological certitude at times bred a cautious patience, at other times it ity. Russian leaders failed to comprehend, for so many East Germans and Eastern Europeans saw rces more as oppressors than liberators; they continued as well to calculate that a war between rival capitalist states was bound to occur and that the capitalist system would before long face another global depression.

Ideology imparted to Soviets and Americans alike a messianic faith in the world-historical roles of their respective nations. On each side of what would soon become the Cold War divide, leaders and ordinary citizens saw their countries acting for much broader purposes than the mere advancement of national interests. Soviets and Americans each, in fact, saw themselves acting out of noble motives – acting to usher humanity into a grand new age of peace, justice, and order. Married to the overwhelming power each nation possessed at a time when much of the world lay prostrate, those mirror-opposite ideological values provided a sure-fire recipe for conflict.

Chapter 2
The origins of the Cold War in Europe, 1945–50

A fragile alliance

A classic marriage of convenience, the wartime alliance between the globe's leading capitalist power and its chief proponent of international proletarian revolution was riddled from the first with tension, mistrust, and suspicion. Beyond the common objective of defeating Nazi Germany, there was little to cement a partnership born of awkward necessity and weighed down by a conflict-ridden past. The United States had, after all, displayed unremitting hostility to the Soviet state ever since the Bolshevik revolution that brought it forth. The Kremlin's rulers, for their part, saw the United States as the ringleader of the capitalist powers that had sought to strangle their regime at infancy. Economic pressure and diplomatic isolation had followed, along with persistent denunciations by American spokesmen of the Soviet government and all it stood for. Washington's belated recognition of the Soviet Union, which came 17 years after the state's establishment, was insufficient to drain the reservoir of bad blood, especially since Stalin's efforts to knit together a common front against Hitler's resurgent Germany in the mid- and late 1930s were met with indifference from the United States and other Western powers. Abandoned yet again by the West, at least from his perspective, and left to face the German wolves alone, Stalin agreed to the Nazi–Soviet pact of 1939 largely as a means of self-protection.

For its part, the United States entered the post-World War I period with nothing but disdain for an unruly, unpredictable regime that had confiscated property, repudiated pre-war debts, and pledged support for working-class revolutions across the globe. American strategists did not fear the conventional military power of the Soviet Union, which was decidedly limited. They worried, rather, about the appeal of the Marxist-Leninist message to downtrodden masses in other lands – as well as in the United States itself – and about the revolutionary insurgencies, and resulting instability, it might spark. Washington, accordingly, laboured to quarantine the communist virus and to isolate its Moscow quartermasters throughout the 1920s and early 1930s. It was like 'having a wicked and disgraceful neighbor', recalled President Herbert Hoover in his memoirs: 'We did not attack him, but we did not give him a certificate of character by inviting him into our homes.' Roosevelt's diplomatic recognition of 1933, prompted by commercial and geopolitical calculations, actually changed very little. The Soviet–American relationship remained frigid right up to Hitler's betrayal of his Soviet ally in June 1941. Before then, the Faustian pact between Germany and Russia had just served to intensify American distaste for Stalin's regime. When the Soviet dictator opportunistically used the German cover to launch aggression against Poland, the Baltic states, and Finland, in 1939–40, anti-Soviet sentiment burgeoned throughout American society.

Following the German invasion of the Soviet Union, ideological antipathy yielded to the dictates of *realpolitik*. Roosevelt and his chief strategists quickly recognized the great geostrategic advantages for the United States of a Soviet Union able to resist the German onslaught; they worried, conversely, about the enhanced power that Germany would gain were it to subdue a country so rich in resources. Consequently, beginning in the summer of 1941, the United States commenced shipping military supplies to the Soviet Union in order to bolster the Red Army's chances. The central dynamic of Roosevelt's policies from June 1941 onward was, as historian Waldo Heinrichs has so aptly put it, 'the conviction that the survival of the Soviet Union was essential for the defeat of Germany and that the defeat of Germany was essential for American security'. Even the inveterately anti-communist Churchill immediately grasped the critical importance of the Soviet Union's survival to the struggle against German aggression. 'If Hitler invaded Hell', he quipped, 'I would make at least a favourable reference to the devil in the House of Commons.' The Americans, the Soviets, and the British thus suddenly found themselves battling a common enemy, a fact formalized with Hitler's declaration of war on the United States two days after Pearl Harbor. More than $11 billion in military aid flowed from the United States to the Soviet Union during the war, serving as the most concrete manifestation of the newfound sense of mutual interest that bound Washington and Moscow together. Meanwhile, the US Government's wartime propaganda machine strained to soften the image of 'Uncle Joe' Stalin and the unsavoury, long-loathed regime he headed.

Precisely how, where, and when to fight their common German adversary, however, were questions that almost immediately generated friction within the Grand Alliance. Stalin pressed his Anglo-American partners to open a major second front against the Germans as quickly as possible so as to relieve the intense military pressure on his own homeland. Yet, despite Roosevelt's promises to do so, the United States and Great Britain chose not to open a major second front until two and a half years after Pearl Harbor, opting instead for less risky, peripheral operations in North Africa and Italy in 1942 and 1943. When Stalin learned in June 1943 that there would be no second front in northwestern Europe for another year, he angrily wrote to Roosevelt that the Soviet Government's 'confidence in its allies . . . is being subjected to severe stress'. He caustically called attention to 'the enormous sacrifices of the Soviet armies, compared with which the sacrifices of the Anglo-American armies are insignificant'. Not surprisingly, Stalin proved wholly unsympathetic to his allies' supply and preparedness problems. They had the luxury of waiting before engaging the full brunt of German armed might; the Russians quite obviously did not. Stalin suspected that his putative allies simply did not assign a particularly high priority to relieving the Soviets; and he was certainly right in the sense that the Americans and British much preferred to have Soviets die in the fight against Hitler if that would allow more of their own soldiers to live. Right up until the launching of the long-postponed Allied invasion of the German-occupied Normandy coast in June 1944, Soviet forces were holding down more than 80% of the *Wehrmacht*'s divisions.

Political disputes also plagued the wartime alliance. None proved more nettlesome than those surrounding the peace terms to be imposed on Germany and the postwar status of Eastern Europe, respectively. At the wartime conference at Tehran, in November 1943, and throughout the following year, Stalin impressed upon Roosevelt and Churchill his conviction that Germany would regain its industrial-military power soon after war's end and once again pose a mortal danger to the Soviet Union. The Russian ruler, accordingly, pushed vigorously for a harsh peace that would strip Germany of both territory and industrial infrastructure. Such an approach would satisfy the Soviet Union's dual need to keep Germany down while extracting from it a sizable contribution to the Soviet rebuilding effort. Roosevelt proved unwilling to commit himself fully to Stalin's punitive proposals, though he did tell Stalin that he, too, saw merit in the permanent dismemberment of Germany. In fact, US experts had not yet decided, at that point, among competing impulses: whether to crush the nation that had precipitated so much carnage; or to treat it magnanimously, using the anticipated occupation period to help fashion a new Germany that could play a constructive role in postwar Europe, with its resources and industry fully utilized in the mammoth task of rehabilitating war-torn Europe. Despite Roosevelt's preliminary nod toward a punitive approach, the issue remained far from settled, as subsequent developments would make painfully clear.

Eastern European questions, which also touched directly on vital Soviet security interests, similarly eluded easy resolution. In theory

and in practice, the Americans and British were reconciled to a
Soviet sphere of influence in Eastern Europe – an Eastern Europe,
in other words, in which the Soviets exercised a predominant
influence. In the crudest version of wartime spheres of influence
diplomacy, in November 1944 Churchill and Stalin tentatively
approved the notorious 'percentages agreements', which purported
to divide much of the Balkans into zones of preponderant British or
Russian influence. Roosevelt never signed on to that *modus
vivendi*, however, since it represented too blatant a violation of the
principles of free and democratic self-determination that formed a
cornerstone of American plans for postwar political order. Yet this
particular square could not be circled. Poland, the country whose
joint invasion by Germany and the Soviet Union had triggered the
European war, well encapsulated the intractable nature of the
problem. Two competing Polish governments vied for international
recognition during the war years: one, headquartered in London,
was led by strongly anti-Soviet Polish nationalists; the other, set up
in the Polish city of Lublin, essentially served as a Soviet puppet
regime. In so polarized a polity, there was no middle ground; hence
little room existed for splitting differences as Roosevelt was wont to
do in domestic political clashes.

At the Yalta Conference of February 1945, Roosevelt, Churchill, and
Stalin tried to resolve some of these basic disputes while also
planning the war's end game. The conference represents the high
point of wartime cooperation, its compromises well reflecting both
the existing balance of power on the ground and the determination
of the 'Big Three' leaders to sustain the spirit of cooperation and
compromise that their unusual alliance's survival required. On the
crucial question of Poland, the Americans and British agreed to
recognize the Soviet-backed Lublin government, provided that
Stalin broaden its representativeness and permit free elections.
Largely as a sop to Roosevelt, who sought a fig leaf to cover this
retreat from one of America's proclaimed war goals – and to
assuage the millions of Americans of Eastern European descent
(most of whom, not insignificantly, were Democratic voters) – Stalin

1. **Churchill, Roosevelt, and Stalin pose for photographers during the Yalta summit of February 1945.**

accepted a Declaration on Liberated Europe. The three leaders pledged, in that public document, to support democratic processes in the establishment of new, representative governments for each of Europe's liberated nations. The Soviet ruler also received the assurance he sought that Germany would be forced to pay reparations, with the tentative figure of $20 billion put on the table, $10 billion of which would be earmarked for the Soviet Union. But final agreement on that issue was deferred to the future. The Soviet commitment to enter the war against Japan within three months after the end of the European War, also negotiated at Yalta, marked a major diplomatic achievement for the United States, as did the formal Soviet agreement to join the United Nations.

From cooperation to conflict, 1945–7

Within weeks of the conference's closing sessions, however, the Yalta spirit was jolted by mounting Anglo-American dissatisfaction with Soviet actions in Eastern Europe. The Soviet Union's crude and brutal repression of non-communist Poles, coupled with its heavy-handed actions in Bulgaria, Romania, and Hungary, all areas recently liberated by the Red Army, struck both Churchill and Roosevelt as violations of the Yalta accords. Churchill urged Roosevelt to make Poland 'a test case between us and the Russians'. The American leader, albeit equally disquieted by Stalin's behaviour, demurred; he remained convinced right up until his last days that a reasonable, give-and-take relationship with the Russians could be preserved. When, on 12 April, Roosevelt succumbed to a massive cerebral hemorrhage, that daunting responsibility fell to the untested and inexperienced Harry S. Truman. How much of a substantive difference the shift in American leadership at so momentous a juncture exerted on the course of US–Soviet relations has remained a subject of intense scholarly debate. Certainly Truman proved more willing than his predecessor to accept the recommendation of hard-line advisers that getting tough with the Russians would help Americans achieve what they wanted. In a revealing, oft-quoted comment, Truman on 20 April said he saw no reason why the United States should not get 85% of what it wanted on important issues. Three days later, he brusquely enjoined Soviet Foreign Minister V. M. Molotov to make sure that his country kept its agreements with regard to Poland. Churchill, too, was growing disgruntled with what he characterized as Soviet brutishness and bullying, setting the stage for a showdown meeting of the Big Three in war-shattered Germany.

In July 1945, two months after the German surrender, US, British, and Soviet leaders made one more effort to hammer out their differences – with mixed results – during the last of the great wartime conferences. The meetings, held in the bombed-out Berlin suburb of Potsdam, dealt with a wide range of issues, including territorial adjustments in East Asia and the specific timing of Soviet entry into the Pacific War. But the thorniest problems, and those that dominated the two-week conference, surrounded the postwar settlements in Eastern Europe and Germany. Stalin gained one of his top diplomatic objectives early in the sessions: Anglo-American recognition of the newly established Warsaw regime. His Grand Alliance partners felt they had no choice but to accept the *fait accompli* of a Soviet-dominated Poland, even with expanded western boundaries rather crudely carved out of former German territory. They balked at comparable recognition of the Soviet-installed governments in Bulgaria and Romania, however. The conferees, instead, established a Council of Foreign Ministers which was to address those and other territorial questions arising from the war in future meetings and to draft peace treaties for the defeated Axis powers.

Germany – the 'big question', as Churchill appropriately labelled it – generated fierce wrangling before an American-sponsored compromise solution saved the proceedings from deadlock, though at the cost of a *de facto* economic division of the country. Reparations, again, emerged as the principal stumbling block. Stalin's insistence on the $10 billion in German reparations that he thought had been agreed upon at Yalta met with firm resistance from Truman and his advisers. The Americans, convinced now that the economic recovery and future prosperity of Western Europe – and of the United States itself – required an economically vibrant Germany, opposed any scheme that would work against that end. Secretary of State James F. Byrnes put forward a compromise offer that the Soviets, in the end, reluctantly accepted. It stipulated that the four occupying powers – the United States, Great Britain, France, and the Soviet Union – would extract reparations primarily from their own designated occupation zones; the Soviets were promised, additionally, some capital equipment from the western zones. Yet those western zones, containing the most highly industrialized and resource-rich sections of the country, would in effect be insulated from Russian influence. Since the Grand Alliance partners were unable to agree upon a unified approach to the German question – the single most contentious diplomatic issue of the war and the issue destined to remain at the heart of the Cold War – they essentially opted for division while trying to retain the pretence of unity. The ramifications of that outcome were far-reaching. It represented an initial step towards the integration of the Western- and Soviet-occupied portions of Germany into separate economic-political systems – and presaged the East–West division of the European continent.

Truman, nonetheless, expressed satisfaction with the portentous decisions reached at Potsdam. 'I like Stalin', he remarked at the

2. Churchill, Truman, and Stalin pose in front of Churchill's residence during the Potsdam Conference of July 1945.

time: 'He is straightforward. Knows what he wants and will compromise when he can't get it.' The American leader's confidence in his ability to get most of what he wanted in future negotiations with his Soviet counterpart rested especially on what the president and his leading advisers saw as Washington's two trump cards: its economic power and its exclusive possession of the atomic bomb. Truman's self-assurance was bolstered significantly when he received word, in the middle of the Potsdam talks, of the successful atomic bomb test that had been carried out in New Mexico. America's 'royal straight flush', as Secretary of War Henry Stimson fondly tagged it, would surely improve the prospects for diplomatic settlements consistent with American interests – or so Truman and his inner circle believed. The atomic bomb blasts over Hiroshima on 6 August and Nagasaki on 9 August, which instantly killed 115,000 and left tens of thousands more dying of radiation sickness, compelled Japan's capitulation. Use of the bomb simultaneously served several American military-diplomatic objectives: it brought the war to a speedy close, saved thousands of American lives by so doing, foreclosed the need for Soviet troops in the Pacific theatre (although not the movement of Soviet troops into Manchuria), and closed the door on any realistic Soviet bid for a role in the postwar occupation of Japan.

Yet, despite the Truman administration's trump cards, Soviet–American relations progressively deteriorated in the months that followed the Japanese surrender. In addition to Eastern Europe and Germany, still the most vexing problems, the former allies clashed over competing visions of how international control of atomic weaponry might be attained, over conflicting interests in the Middle East and Eastern Mediterranean, over the question of US economic aid, and over the Soviet role in Manchuria. Although some compromises were forged in the various meetings of the Council of Foreign Ministers, 1946 marked the demise of the Grand Alliance and the beginning of a fully fledged Cold War.

Throughout that year, the Truman administration and its principal

Western European allies came increasingly to view Stalin's Russia as an opportunistic bully with what seemed a voracious appetite for additional territories, resources, and concessions. George F. Kennan, the senior US diplomat in Moscow, articulated and lent weight to that assessment in his landmark 'long telegram' of 22 February 1946. Soviet hostility to the capitalist world was as immutable as it was inevitable, Kennan emphasized, the result of the unfortunate merger of traditional Russian insecurity with Marxist-Leninist dogma. He argued that the Kremlin's rulers had imposed an oppressive totalitarian regime on the Soviet people, and now used the presumed threat posed by external enemies to justify a continuation of the internal tyranny that kept them in power. Kennan's advice was pointed: eschew accommodation, which would never work in any case; concentrate, instead, upon checking the spread of Soviet power and influence. The Kremlin, he insisted, would yield only to superior force. On 5 March, Winston Churchill, now out of power, publicly added his voice to the swelling anti-Soviet chorus. In Fulton, Missouri, with an evidently approving Harry Truman sharing the podium, the British wartime leader railed: 'From Stettin in the Baltic to Trieste in the Adriatic, an iron curtain has descended across the Continent.' Christian civilization itself, Churchill warned, was now endangered by communist expansionism.

Soviet behaviour alone did not warrant the degree of alarm emanating from Western capitals, and certainly not the doomsday scenarios being sketched in some American quarters. The Stalinist regime did press its advantages at nearly every turn, to be sure. It imposed subservient governments on Poland, Romania, and Bulgaria; carved out an exclusive sphere of influence in its occupation zone in east Germany; initially refused to remove its troops from Iran, precipitating the first major Cold War crisis in March 1946; pressed Turkey aggressively for concessions, even massing troops along the Bulgarian border in an effort at intimidation; pillaged Manchuria; and more. Yet the Soviets also allowed relatively free elections in Hungary and Czechoslovakia, cooperated in the formation of representative governments in Finland and Austria, continued to engage in spirited negotiations with the Western powers through the institutionalized Council of Foreign Ministers, and even acted to restrain the powerful communist parties in Italy, France, and elsewhere in Western Europe. Soviet behaviour, in short, allowed for more subtle and balanced interpretations than those offered by Kennan and Churchill.

Actually, what US and UK analysts feared most was neither Soviet behaviour per se nor the hostile intentions that might underlie such behaviour. Nor were they unduly concerned about Soviet military capabilities, at least not in the short run. Top American and British military experts judged the Soviet Union too weak to risk war against the United States; they considered a Red Army attack on Western Europe, in particular, as highly improbable. What induced apprehension among American and British policy-makers was, rather, the prospect that the Soviet Union might capitalize on and benefit from the socioeconomic distress and accompanying political upheavals that continued to mark the postwar world. Those conditions had abetted the rise of the left worldwide, a phenomenon most disturbingly reflected in the growing popularity of communist parties in Western Europe, but also manifested in the surge of revolutionary, anti-colonial, and radical nationalist movements across the Third World. The severe social and economic disruptions of the war made communism seem an appealing alternative to many of the world's people. Western foreign and defence ministries feared that local communist parties and indigenous revolutionary movements would ally with and defer to the Soviet Union, a state whose legitimacy and prestige had been burnished substantially by its central role in the anti-fascist crusade. The Kremlin, consequently, could augment its power and extend its reach without even needing to risk direct military action. For US strategists, the frightening shadow of 1940–1 loomed. Another hostile power, armed once again with an alien, threatening ideology, might gain control over Eurasia, thereby tipping the scales of world power against the United States, denying it access to important markets and resources, and placing political and economic freedom at home in jeopardy.

Drawing lines

To meet those grave, if diffuse, threats, the United States moved with dizzying speed during the first half of 1947 to implement a strategy aimed simultaneously at containing the Soviet Union *and* reducing the appeal of communism. A British initiative, necessitated by London's declining power and deepening financial woes, propelled the first critical step in the US diplomatic offensive. On 21 February, the British Government informed the State Department that it could no longer afford to provide economic and military assistance to Greece and Turkey. American officials quickly determined that the United States must assume Britain's former role so as to block the possible spread of Soviet influence into the eastern Mediterranean – and into the oil-rich Middle East beyond. To gain support from a cost-conscious Congress and a public disinclined to accept new international obligations, Truman, on 12 March, delivered a forceful address to Congress in which he asked for $400 million in economic and military support for the beleaguered governments of Greece and Turkey.

On one level, the United States was simply acting here to fill a power vacuum created by the contraction of British power. The right-wing Greek Government was fighting a civil war against indigenous communists supplied by communist Yugoslavia. The Turks, for their part, faced persistent Russian pressure for concessions in the Dardanelles. Moscow and its allies thus stood to benefit from the British withdrawal, an unsettling prospect that the American initiative aimed to foreclose. What is particularly significant about the Truman Doctrine, however, is less that basic fact of power politics than the manner in which the American president chose to present his aid proposal. Using hyperbolic language, Manichean imagery, and deliberate simplification to

The Truman Doctrine

'At the present moment in world history', Truman told Congress in his appeal for the Greek-Turkish aid package, 'nearly every nation must choose between alternative ways of life.' After cataloguing the perfidies of the Soviet Union, though never directly naming it, Truman famously concluded with the exhortation that 'it must be the policy of the United States to support free peoples who are resisting attempted subjugation by armed minorities or by outside pressure'. That breathtakingly open-ended commitment was quickly dubbed the Truman Doctrine.

strengthen his public appeal, Truman was vying to build a public and Congressional consensus not just behind this particular commitment but behind a more activist American foreign policy – a policy that would be at once anti-Soviet and *anti-communist*. The Truman Doctrine thus amounted to a declaration of ideological Cold War along with a declaration of geopolitical Cold War. Yet ambiguities abounded, and they would reverberate throughout the entire Cold War era. What, precisely, was the nature of the threat that justified so full-scale a commitment? Was it the potential growth of Soviet power? Or was it the spread of a set of ideas antithetical to American values? The two, quite distinct, dangers merged imperceptibly in US thinking.

Three months after Truman's epochal speech, the United States publicly announced the second major phase of its diplomatic offensive. Secretary of State George C. Marshall, during a Harvard University commencement address, promised US aid to all European countries willing to coordinate their recovery efforts. The enemies that the United States sought to combat with what was soon labelled the Marshall Plan were the hunger, poverty, and demoralization fuelling the rise of the left in postwar Europe, a set of circumstances abetted by stalled recovery efforts and exacerbated by the most severe winter for the past 80 years. British Foreign Minister Ernest Bevin and French Foreign Minister Georges Bidault responded immediately and enthusiastically to Marshall's overture. They organized a meeting of interested European states that soon came up with a set of organizing principles to govern the proposed US aid programme. British, French, and other Western European governments sensed a golden opportunity to help alleviate serious economic problems, counter local communist parties, and thwart Soviet expansion. They shared, in short, many of the Truman administration's concerns about the dangers inherent in the postwar environment, even if Europeans tended to be less ideologically fixated than their American counterparts in their understanding of the threat. Western European leaders plainly welcomed – and invited – a more active US policy towards and stronger presence in postwar Europe because this dovetailed with their own economic, political, and security needs. The Marshall Plan eventually provided $13 billion in assistance to Western Europe, helping to jump-start economic recovery there, encourage European economic integration, and restore an important market for American goods. Stalin, fearful that the European Recovery Program would be used to loosen Russia's grip on its satellites, forbade Eastern European participation. Soviet Foreign Minister Molotov walked out of the Paris organizing conference with a stern warning that the Marshall Plan 'would split Europe into two groups of states'.

A decisive reorientation of its German policy formed another integral part of the Truman administration's diplomatic offensive. American policy-makers deemed the participation of the western occupation zones of Germany in the Marshall Plan to be essential to the plan's prospects, since German industry and resources constituted the indispensable engines of European economic growth. Even before the Marshall Plan's unveiling, the United States had moved to boost coal production within the by-then merged American and British occupation zones. Washington planners were convinced that global peace and prosperity, as well as the security and economic well-being of the United States, depended upon European economic recovery, and that those overriding policy goals required, in turn, a strong, economically revivified Germany. Those goals militated against any diplomatic compromise with the Soviet Union on the all-important German question. Secretary of State Marshall's insistence on German participation in the European Recovery Program essentially killed any lingering prospects for a four-power accord on Germany, and led directly to the acrimonious collapse of the November 1947 meetings of the Council of Foreign Ministers. 'We really do not want nor intend to accept German unification in any terms that the Russians might agree to', a high-ranking American diplomat privately admitted. Preferring to divide the country rather than to run the risk of a reunified Germany that might over time align itself with the Soviet Union or, almost as bad, adopt a neutralist stance, the United States, Great Britain, and France, in early 1948, took the first steps towards the creation of an independent West German state. British Ambassador Lord Inverchapel correctly observed that the Americans believed that the 'division of Germany and the absorption of the two parts into rival Eastern and Western spheres is preferable to the creation of a no-man's land on the border of an expanding Soviet hegemony'.

Given Stalin's oft-stated concerns about the revival of German power, those Western policy initiatives virtually ensured a vigorous Soviet reaction. US officials certainly expected as much – and they were not disappointed. In September 1947, at a conference in Poland, the Soviets established the Communist Information Bureau (Cominform) as a means of tightening control over both their satellite states in Eastern Europe and the communist parties of Western Europe. Decrying the Marshall Plan as part of a concerted strategy to forge a Western alliance that would serve as a 'jumping-off place for attacking the Soviet Union', chief Russian delegate Andrei Zhdanov said the world was now divided into 'two camps'.

A Soviet-sponsored coup in Czechoslovakia, in February 1948, followed. It led to the dismissal of all non-communist ministers from the government, and left respected Foreign Minister Jan Masaryk dead in its wake – in highly suspicious circumstances. Along with heavy-handed repression of the non-communist opposition in Hungary, the Czech coup heralded a much tougher Soviet stance within its 'camp' and helped crystallize Europe's East–West split.

Then, on 24 June 1948, Stalin threw the hammer down. In response to the Anglo-American-French rehabilitation and consolidation of West Germany, the Soviets suddenly halted all allied ground access to West Berlin. By isolating the western enclave in that divided city, located 125 miles within Soviet-occupied eastern Germany, Stalin aimed to expose his adversaries' vulnerability, thereby derailing the establishment of the separate West German state he so feared. Truman responded by initiating a round-the-clock airlift of supplies and fuel to the 2 million embattled residents of West Berlin in one of the most storied, and tension-filled, episodes of the early Cold War. In May 1949, Stalin finally called off what had turned into an ineffectual blockade – and a public relations disaster. The clumsy Soviet riposte succeeded only in deepening the East–West split, inflaming public opinion in the United States and Western Europe, and destroying whatever shred of hope still existed for a German settlement acceptable to all four occupying powers. In September 1949, the Western powers created the Federal Republic of Germany. One month later, the Soviets established the German Democratic Republic in their occupation zone. Europe's Cold War lines were now clearly demarcated, the division of Germany between west and east mirroring the broader division of Europe into American-led and Soviet-led spheres.

A number of top Western European diplomats, none more determinedly than British Foreign Minister Ernest Bevin, believed that the burgeoning European–American connection could only be cemented through a formal trans-Atlantic security agreement.

Towards that end, the burly former labour leader became the prime mover behind the formation of the Brussels Pact of April 1948. That mutual security agreement between Britain, France, the Netherlands, Belgium, and Luxembourg, Bevin hoped, could serve as the basis for a broader Western alliance. What he sought was a mechanism that would simultaneously draw the Americans more fully into Western European affairs, assuage French anxieties about the revival of Germany, and deter the Soviets – or, as a popular saying crudely but not inaccurately put it: a means 'to keep the Americans in, the Soviets out, and the Germans down.' The North Atlantic Treaty Organization (NATO) met the needs identified by Bevin – and by a Truman administration intent upon adding a security anchor to its developing containment strategy. Signed in Washington on 4 April 1949, NATO brought together the Brussels signatories, Italy, Denmark, Norway, Portugal, Canada, and the United States in a mutual security pact. Each of the member-states consented to treat an attack on one or more as an attack on all. This commitment represented an historic reversal for the United States of one of the defining traditions of its foreign policy. Not since the alliance with France of the late 18th century had Washington formed an entangling alliance or merged its own security needs so seamlessly with those of other sovereign states.

The sphere of influence, or 'empire', that the United States forged in postwar Europe stands as a product of its fears more than its ambitions. It was a product, moreover, of a convergence of interest between US and Western European elites. Indeed, the latter deserve recognition as co-authors of what historian Geir Lundestad has termed America's 'empire by invitation'. Important distinctions obtain, in this regard, between a Soviet empire that was essentially imposed on much of Eastern Europe and an American empire that resulted from a partnership born of common security fears and overlapping economic needs.

Although an undeniably crucial development in the onset of the Cold War, the division of Europe into hostile spheres of influence forms only part of our story. Had the Cold War been restricted to a competition for power and influence in Europe alone, that story would have played out very differently than it ultimately did. The next chapter, consequently, shifts the geographical focus to Asia, the Cold War's second major theatre of the early postwar era.

Chapter 3
Towards 'Hot War' in Asia, 1945–50

Asia became the second major theatre of the Cold War – and the place where the Cold War first turned hot. Europe, of course, generated more controversy and received far more attention from the United States and the Soviet Union, emerging as the principal focus of tensions between the former allies in the immediate aftermath of World War II. Each identified interests there that appeared vital both to its short-term and long-term security needs and economic well-being. The development and hardening of an American sphere of influence in Western Europe and a corresponding Soviet sphere in Eastern Europe forms the very essence of the Cold War's opening phase, as the previous chapter has argued, with Germany serving as ground zero of the Cold War. Yet open conflict between East and West was averted in Europe – in the late 1940s and throughout the four decades that followed. Asia, where Washington and Moscow also had important, if decidedly less vital, interests, proved not so fortunate. As many as 6 million soldiers and civilians would ultimately lose their lives in Cold War-related conflicts in Korea and Indo-China. It was the outbreak of the Korean War in June 1950, moreover, that precipitated the first direct military showdown between US and communist forces and, as much as any other single event, turned the Cold War into a worldwide struggle.

Japan: from mortal enemy to Cold War ally

World War II catalysed far-reaching changes across the breadth of the Asian continent. Japan's stunning string of conquests in the war's early months – in Singapore, in Malaya, in Burma, in the Philippines, in the Dutch East Indies, in French Indo-China, and elsewhere – capsized the Western colonial system in East Asia, at least temporarily, while simultaneously puncturing the myth of white racial superiority on which Western rule ultimately rested. 'The British Empire in the Far East depended on prestige', observed an Australian diplomat at the time. 'This prestige has been completely shattered.' The ensuing Japanese occupation of British, French, Dutch, and American colonial possessions, rationalized by the effective, if self-serving, 'Asia for the Asians' slogan, accelerated the growth of nationalist consciousness among Asian peoples. It also set the stage for the nationalist revolutions that would erupt at war's end. The vacuums of power left by the precipitous surrender of Japan on 14 August 1945 gave aspirant nationalists the time to organize, mobilize, and win popular support for the indigenous alternatives to Japanese, and Western, dominance that they hurriedly sought to construct.

The epic struggles for national freedom and independence mounted by Asian and other Third World peoples in the aftermath of World War II rank among the most powerful historical forces of the 20th century. Those struggles, it bears emphasizing, were quite distinct from the temporally overlapping contest for power and influence being waged by the United States and the Soviet Union, and doubtless would have transpired with or without a Cold War. Yet the latter conflict did occur, and its totalizing character inevitably shaped the temper, pace, and ultimate outcome of the former. Decolonization and the Cold War were fated to become inextricably linked, each shaping and being shaped by the other, in Asia as elsewhere.

As the postwar era dawned, neither the United States nor the Soviet

Union seemed to recognize that the old order in East Asia had been fatally undermined by the Pacific War or to appreciate the extent to which the nationalist currents it unleashed would fundamentally change Asian societies. The Soviets initially pursued a characteristically opportunistic yet cautious policy in East Asia, one wholly consistent with their actions in postwar Europe. Stalin sought to reclaim all territory once held by Czarist Russia, to re-establish economic concessions in Manchuria and Outer Mongolia, and to ensure Soviet security along the 4,150-mile Sino-Soviet border. Those aims pointed towards the need to keep China friendly but weak – and preferably divided – to avoid any major clashes with the Western powers, and to restrain the revolutionary impulses of local communist parties. For its part, the United States advanced a more wide-ranging and ambitious foreign policy agenda, predicated upon defanging Japan, turning the Pacific into an American lake, transforming China into a dependable and stable ally, and fostering a moderate solution to the colonial problem.

First and foremost, though, US planners considered it imperative that Japan never again be allowed to threaten the peace of the region. To that end, Washington was determined that it, and it alone, would oversee the postwar occupation and restructuring of Japan. The American goal was as straightforward as it was ambitious: to use its power to remake Japanese society by destroying all vestiges of militarism while helping to foster the development of liberal, democratic institutions. To a remarkable extent, the United States succeeded. Under the supervision of the imperious General Douglas MacArthur, the American occupation regime spurred a wide-ranging set of reforms: extensive land reform was initiated, labour laws passed that provided for collective bargaining rights and the establishment of unions, educational improvements enacted, and equal rights granted to women. The new constitution of May 1947 formally renounced war, prohibited the maintenance of armed forces, and laid down the principles for a system of representative, democratic governance under the rule of law. It was, in the words of one historian, 'perhaps the single most exhaustively planned operation of massive and externally directed political change in world history'.

Unlike the case of Germany, which was governed directly by four different powers and divided among them for administrative-political purposes, the occupation in Japan was dominated by a single power that ruled indirectly, preferring to exert its will through close collaboration with the pragmatic Japanese governmental bureaucracy. Japan, of course, also in contradistinction to Germany, was left fully intact as a sovereign national entity.

Yet, for all those salient differences, US officials essentially treated Japan, especially after 1947, as the Asian analogue to (West) Germany: a nation whose advanced industrial infrastructure, skilled workforce, and technological prowess made it both the indispensable engine of regional economic growth and a Cold War strategic asset of incalculable value. As East–West tensions in Europe mounted, the US occupation regime in Japan shifted from a concentration on reforming and demilitarizing a former enemy state to a preoccupation with facilitating its rapid economic recovery. A stable, economically vibrant, pro-American Japan was judged by US strategists to be just as essential to overall US policy objectives in postwar Asia as a stable, economically vibrant, pro-American Germany was to overall US policy objectives in postwar Europe. In each case, geopolitical and economic goals were woven into a seamless web. American experts considered Japan the most important nation in Asia because of its potential as the engine of East Asian economic recovery and because of its intrinsic strategic value. From 1947 onwards, the Truman administration's over-riding Asian policy goal was to orient a stable, prosperous Japan to the West. If Tokyo fell under communist influence, the Joint Chiefs of Staff warned Truman, the 'USSR would gain, thereby, an additional war-making potential equal to 25% of her capacity'. In December 1949, Secretary of State Dean Acheson similarly framed

Japan's strategic importance in terms of the overall power balance between East and West. 'Were Japan added to the communist bloc', he emphasized, 'the Soviets would acquire skilled manpower and industrial potential capable of significantly altering the balance of world power.'

In view of the enormity of the perceived stakes, US officials were agreed that protecting Japan from any external communist threat and simultaneously inoculating it from any possible internal contagion stood as America's cardinal regional priorities. Yet, despite the noteworthy early successes of the occupation, they remained apprehensive about the future, fearing in particular that developments across the China Sea might undercut the prospects for a revitalized Japan anchored firmly to the West. As the Chinese communists gained the upper hand by the late 1940s in China's ongoing civil war, US analysts fretted that Japan's traditional reliance on China as its principal overseas market might over time draw it into the communist orbit. After all, as Japan's Prime Minister Shigeru Yoshida put it: 'Whether China is red or green, China is a natural market.' The orientation of Japan and the future of China were problems not easily separated.

The Communist triumph in China

The proclamation of the People's Republic of China on 1 October 1949 represented not just a monumental personal triumph for Mao Zedong and the other leaders of a Chinese Communist movement that had been routed, hunted, and nearly extinguished by Chiang Kai-shek's ruling Guomindang Party two decades earlier. It also signified a fundamental shift in the nature and locus of the Cold War – with weighty strategic, ideological, and domestic political implications.

During World War II, the Roosevelt administration had bolstered the Chiang regime with substantial amounts of military and economic assistance, though never enough to satisfy the demanding generalissimo. Roosevelt wanted to turn the Chinese military into an effective anti-Japanese fighting force and the Chiang regime into a reliable American ally, one capable of assuming a stabilizing and balancing role in postwar Asian affairs. To further those objectives, Roosevelt met with Chiang at Cairo in 1943, before and immediately following the Big Three summit conference at Teheran to which the Chinese leader was not invited. During their Cairo discussions, the American president flattered Chiang by symbolically elevating China to great power status; Roosevelt subsequently talked about China as one of the 'Four Policemen' that, along with the United States, the Soviet Union, and Great Britain, would help maintain peace after the war. He boosted China in this manner partly to cement Sino-American ties, partly to compensate for the additional material assistance that Chiang requested but Washington was unable to provide, and partly to keep China in the war, thereby precluding the possibility of a disastrous separate peace between China and Japan. But neither Roosevelt's symbolic gestures nor the military and diplomatic missions he dispatched with some regularity to the Guomindang's wartime capital in Chongqing proved sufficient to coax a meaningful military contribution from Chiang's troops.

By 1944, American diplomats on the scene increasingly disparaged the long-term prospects for a regime mired in corruption, venality, and incompetence. For its part, the Guomindang, or Nationalist, government was convinced that the chief threat to its existence emanated not from the Japanese, whom their American allies would surely defeat with or without significant Chinese help, but from the Chinese Communists. Under Mao's capable leadership, the latter had blossomed into a formidable military and political force during the years of Japanese occupation, and had gained control of vast portions of northern and central China. Rather than expending men and materiel battling the Japanese invaders, Chiang and his inner circle chose to husband precious resources for what they expected to be an inevitable showdown with the communists after the war.

3. Mao Zedong, Chinese leader and chairman of the Chinese Communist Party.

At the Yalta Conference, in February 1945, Roosevelt looked to an unusual source for a solution to America's policy dilemma in China. Thoroughly disillusioned by Chiang's unwillingness to fight, he sought and gained a Soviet commitment to enter the war against Japan within three months after the end of hostilities in Europe. Stalin's price for that gesture – Roosevelt's promise to help the Soviets regain czarist-era concessions in Manchuria and Outer Mongolia – proved acceptable to a US president who attached great value to minimizing the loss of American lives in what was expected to be the extremely bloody denouement of the Pacific War. On 14 August, Chiang assented to those Soviet concessions in the officially entitled Sino-Soviet Treaty of Friendship and Mutual Assistance in return for Moscow's recognition of the legal sovereignty of his government.

The Chinese Communists, not surprisingly, felt betrayed by their presumed ideological compatriots. Plainly, Stalin's calculation of Russia's national interests superseded any sentimental attachment he had to the cause of fellow communist revolutionaries. The Soviet ruler, in fact, preferred a weak, divided China to a strong, unified China – no matter who was in charge. He wanted the Chinese Communists to remain dependent on and subservient to Moscow, sensing risks in an intensely nationalistic movement that, were it to gain power, might seek to assert sovereignty over all Chinese territory, thereby jeopardizing the sphere of influence he craved. The reflexively risk-averse Soviet dictator also wanted to avoid provoking the United States. Stalin was content to loot Manchuria, which Soviet troops proceeded to do following their entry into northeast China in August 1945, and to solidify Moscow's newly acquired commercial gains there and in other border areas. The needs of Mao, a man Stalin viewed as an obstreperous, hard-to-control upstart leading a group of 'margarine' communists, took a back seat to the needs of the Soviet fatherland.

Following the Japanese surrender, the political situation in China progressively deteriorated. Like Chiang, Mao considered a genuine peace between the communists and the Guomindang to be highly unlikely, and a civil war inevitable. In an inner-party directive of 11 August, he instructed Communist Party cadres and military leaders to 'gather our forces in order to prepare for the civil war'. Throughout the autumn of 1945, communist and nationalist troops clashed in northeast China, with Chiang aggressively using US equipment and transport in an effort to dislodge communist forces.

US hopes for a unified, peaceful, pro-American China steadily faded. General Albert Wedemeyer, commander of the small contingent of US forces in China, urged Washington to back Chiang unreservedly. 'If China were to become a puppet state of the Soviets', he prophesied, 'which is exactly what a Chinese communist victory would mean, then Soviet Russia would practically control the continents of Europe and Asia.' Other American analysts disagreed with such alarmism. Convinced that Chiang could not defeat the Chinese Communists militarily, and that only a negotiated peace between the communists and nationalists would avert a civil war sure to destabilize China and wreak havoc with American policy goals, they insisted that Chiang needed to compromise with, not seek to crush, his political rivals. At the end of 1945, President Truman dispatched General George C. Marshall, the most respected and accomplished US military man of his generation, to China to mediate a peaceful resolution of the conflict.

Early in 1946, Marshall succeeded in arranging a temporary truce, but it soon unravelled. The American general's attempts to fashion a compromise settlement between Chiang and Mao ultimately rested on the illusion that power could somehow be shared in a coalition government that would include communists and nationalists. Despite Marshall's impartiality, those efforts foundered on the intractable differences between the two parties, neither of which trusted or was willing to share power with the other. By the end of 1946, Marshall determined, correctly, that this struggle could only be resolved through the force of arms, and that it was a contest Chiang could not possibly win. The Truman administration continued to provide aid to the Chiang regime – a total of $2.8 billion between the Japanese surrender and 1950 – but more to protect its political flanks from assault by nationalist Chinese supporters in the Congress and the media, the so-called China lobby, than in the conviction that US support alone would enable the inept Guomindang forces to prevail. By the end of 1948, defeat turned into rout, with Chiang and his inner circle fleeing the mainland for the island of Taiwan. Mao's dramatic declaration of the new People's Republic of China from Beijing's Gate of Heavenly Peace, in October 1949, merely formalized an outcome that most informed observers had long before anticipated.

The communist victory in the Chinese civil war, although primarily the product of complex forces internal to China, carried unavoidable Cold War ramifications. A nationalist regime backed by the United States – in spite of the rocky, mistrust-laden relationship between Washington and Chiang – had been defeated by a communist movement backed by the Soviet Union – in spite of the rocky, mistrust-laden relationship between Moscow and Mao. Asian, European, and other interested bystanders instantly assessed the outcome of the Chinese civil war as a major defeat for the West and an epochal victory both for the Soviet Union and for world communism. So, too, did critics of Truman at home who blasted the president for losing China through ill-conceived, if not traitorous, actions. For their part, Truman administration planners viewed the communist triumph in China with some degree of equanimity, judging it a disappointing setback for the United States rather than an unmitigated strategic disaster. Secretary of State Dean Acheson and his top State Department lieutenants, first of all, did not consider impoverished, war-ravaged China to be a critical ingredient in the overall balance of world power – at least not for the foreseeable future. Hence the stakes in China were not on a par with those in play in Europe and Japan – or even the Middle East. Second, they concluded that a Communist China did not necessarily translate into a unified, Sino-Soviet, anti-American bloc. Senior US strategists believed that conflicting geopolitical ambitions worked against the development of strong bonds between Stalin's Soviet Union and Mao's China. Finally, they were hopeful that Beijing's desperate need for economic assistance might give the United States the opening it needed to drive a wedge between the two communist powers.

Some historians believe that the United States actually squandered a unique opportunity to develop friendly, or at least businesslike, relations with China at this important juncture. Certain elements within the Chinese Communist government did desire a positive relationship with the United States so as to gain needed reconstruction aid and to avoid overdependence on the Kremlin. On the American side, Acheson thought that, once the 'dust settled', Washington could extend diplomatic recognition to Beijing and salvage what it could from the wreckage of the civil war. Recent Chinese evidence suggests, however, that such a 'lost opportunity' never really existed. Driven by a determination to remake China, a determination fuelled by his fury at the Western imperialists who had for so long defiled China, and needing an external foe to help mobilize popular support for his grand revolutionary ambitions at home, Mao gravitated naturally towards the Soviet camp. He thus rejected all suggestions from underlings that Beijing offer an olive branch to Washington. Instead, the Chinese leader travelled to Moscow in December 1949 and, despite the chilly reception he received from a still wary Stalin, managed to negotiate a treaty of friendship and alliance with the Soviet Union. The Sino-Soviet treaty obligated each power to come to the aid of the other if attacked by a third party, serving as perhaps the most ominous symbol of a Cold War now firmly rooted on Asian soil.

The Cold War comes to Southeast Asia

Just as the Chinese civil war became inextricably entangled with the Cold War, so too did the independence struggles in postwar Southeast Asia. Indigenous nationalists and European colonial powers alike sought to gain international legitimacy and needed external backing by invoking the East–West contest, cloaking their respective causes in Cold War garb in order to coax diplomatic and material support from one or another of the superpowers. The ensuing 'globalization' of these local disputes established a pattern that was to become common throughout the entire Cold War era. Neither the United States nor the Soviet Union at first identified vital interests in Southeast Asia or detected a meaningful connection between local power struggles in this distant corner of the globe and the far more significant diplomatic tussles in Europe. Yet the challenges posed by the two areas could not so easily be separated and, by the late 1940s, coincident with the Chinese Communist triumph, Washington and Moscow increasingly looked at Southeast Asia as another important theatre of East–West conflict.

Prior to World War II, the Soviet Union had never devoted much attention to Southeast Asia. It was surprisingly slow, moreover, to recognize the geopolitical advantages it might reap from aligning itself with anti-Western, revolutionary insurgencies there, whether communist-led or not. Washington, like Moscow, paid scant attention to Southeast Asia in the immediate post-World War II period. It moved quickly to divest itself of its own colonial possession in the area, presiding over the orderly transfer of sovereignty to an independent, pro-American government in the Philippines in July 1946. The Americans retained a visible presence in the Philippine islands, to be sure, demanding extensive base rights which helped secure for the US military a formidable naval and air capability that could be projected throughout the Pacific. Aside from those military bases, and a general desire here, as elsewhere, for peace, stability, and a more open trading regime, US interests in Southeast Asia seemed minimal.

The Truman administration encouraged the British, French, and Dutch to follow its Philippine lead by transferring gradually the reins of civil authority to local, pro-Western elites while maintaining some degree of commercial, security, and political influence in former colonies. That formula struck American experts as best suited to the long-term peace and prosperity that US interests here, as elsewhere, required. The British, under the progressive Labour Government of Prime Minister Clement Attlee, adopted the same basic formula, negotiating the peaceful devolution of power in most of their Asian possessions. India and Pakistan became independent in 1947, Burma and Ceylon in 1948. The French and the Dutch, on the other hand, were determined to regain control of Indo-China and the East Indies, each of which the Japanese had seized and occupied during the war. Their unwillingness to bow to what the Anglo-American powers rightly recognized as an irreversible historical force not only caused much needless bloodshed, but added a distinct Cold War coloration to the two most contentious decolonization struggles of the early postwar era.

The United States initially strove to maintain a public posture of impartiality and neutrality towards the French-Vietnamese and Dutch-Indonesian disputes. It took pains to avoid alienating either European colonialists or Asian nationalists, so far as possible, while retaining some influence with each. Yet the Truman administration, in practice, tilted towards its European allies from the outset; it considered France and the Netherlands too valuable to the emerging anti-Soviet coalition to risk antagonizing by waving an

Ho Chi Minh

The legendary Vietnamese nationalist leader was born in 1890 to a relatively privileged and educated Vietnamese family. Unwilling to work for the French colonial regime, he left his home in 1912, settling eventually within the Vietnamese exile community in Paris. Ho joined the French Communist Party in 1920, received ideological and organizational training in the Soviet Union, worked as an agent of the Communist International (Comintern) during the 1920s and 1930s, and founded the Indochina Communist Party in 1930. Returning to Vietnam in 1941, after an absence of nearly 30 years, Ho organized the Viet Minh as a nationalist alternative to French and Japanese rule. On 2 September 1945, in the wake of the Japanese surrender, he proclaimed an independent Democratic Republic of Vietnam.

anti-colonial banner. Both Ho Chi Minh and Sukarno, the respective leaders of the Vietnamese and Indonesian nationalist movements, appealed for US support on the grounds of America's wartime pledges favouring self-determination. Both were disappointed when their appeals fell on deaf ears, and were resentful of Washington's indirect support for the imperial sovereigns they were seeking to topple.

By 1948–9, a series of interconnected, extra-regional factors led US officials to become more worried about, and involved in, Southeast Asian affairs. The raging colonial conflicts in Indo-China and the East Indies, together with a communist-led insurgency in British Malaya, proved a significant drag on Western European recovery. The primary products of Southeast Asia had traditionally contributed to the economic vitality, and dollar-earning capacity, of Great Britain, France, and the Netherlands. Unsettled conditions in Southeast Asia, however, not only precluded such a contribution but absorbed money, resources, and manpower required for the Marshall Plan and incipient Atlantic alliance – America's top Cold War priorities. US experts were convinced that Japan's recovery, too, was being hampered by the political instability and resulting economic stagnation in Southeast Asia. Japan needed overseas markets for its economic survival. Yet, with the consolidation of communist control in China, US policy-makers actively discouraged trade with the Chinese mainland, Japan's largest pre-war market, for fear that close commercial links might draw Tokyo and Beijing together politically. Substitute markets in Southeast Asia appeared the most promising answer to Japan's export dilemma; but the region's political and economic turmoil first had to be quelled. The emergence of a communist regime in Asia's most populous country constituted the other major external factor propelling a more activist US posture in Southeast Asia. US analysts feared China's expansionist proclivities; the possibility that it might use its military power to gain control over parts of Southeast Asia posed one threat, the likelihood that it would provide support for revolutionary insurgencies another.

In response to those problems, the United States made a series of new commitments to Southeast Asia aimed at simultaneously spurring the political stabilization of the area and containing the Chinese threat. Most significantly, it abandoned its quasi-neutral approach to the Indo-China dispute in favour of a policy of open support for the French, officially recognizing, in February 1950, the French-installed puppet regime headed by former Emperor Bao Dai and promising direct military support. The Truman administration also stepped up its aid to British forces battling the communist insurrection in Malaya. Washington promised as well economic and technical aid to the governments of Burma, Thailand, the Philippines, and Indonesia. The latter achieved independence in December 1949, after a hard-fought struggle with the Dutch, partly because the United States abandoned its quasi-neutral status there as well, though in this case to pressure a European ally to recognize what appeared a moderate, and decidedly non-communist, nationalist movement.

Where the United States perceived dangers, its Cold War adversaries sensed opportunities. Strong fraternal bonds, and parallel interests, helped forge a common front between Mao, Stalin, and Ho Chi Minh. The latter, a three-decade-long communist with extensive service in the Communist International, as well as a Vietnamese patriot of impeccable credentials, made a secret trip to Beijing, in January 1950, in an effort to gain diplomatic recognition and material support from China's new rulers. The next month, he travelled to the Soviet Union and made a personal appeal for support to Stalin – and to Mao, who was himself in Moscow at the time hammering out what became the Sino-Soviet treaty of alliance. Ho's efforts met with success. In early 1950, both Moscow and Beijing extended formal diplomatic recognition to Ho's fledgling Democratic Republic of Vietnam; Mao shortly thereafter authorized the provision of military equipment and training to his Viet Minh fighters. The Chinese leader believed that by strengthening the Vietnamese communists he could help safeguard China's southern border, diminish the threat posed by the

United States and its allies, and lay claim to a central role in the anti-imperialist struggle in Asia. Mao created a Chinese Military Advisory Group which he dispatched to northern Vietnam to help organize Viet Minh resistance to the French and lend expertise to its overall military strategy. Mao's interest in the Viet Minh cause, and his support for it, increased after the outbreak of war on the Korean peninsula in June 1950, just as US interest in and support for the French military effort intensified with the onset of the Korean conflict.

War comes to Korea

In the early morning hours of 25 June 1950, an attacking force of close to 100,000 North Koreans, armed with over 1,400 artillery pieces and accompanied by 126 tanks, crossed the 38th parallel into South Korea. The unexpected invasion ushered in a new and much more dangerous phase of the Cold War, not just in Asia but globally. Certain that the attack could only have occurred with the backing of the Soviet Union and China – a correct assessment, as now-available evidence confirms – and convinced that it heralded a bolder and more aggressive worldwide offensive by the communist powers, the Truman administration responded vigorously. It immediately dispatched US naval and air forces to Korea in order to stem the North Korean advance and bolster South Korean defences. When that initial intervention proved insufficient, the administration dispatched US combat troops, which became part of an international force owing to the UN's condemnation of the North Korean invasion. 'The attack upon Korea makes it plain beyond all doubt', declared Truman in a 27 June address to the American people, 'that Communism has passed beyond the use of subversion to conquer independent nations and will use armed invasion and war.' He also revealed, in that same speech, that he was ordering the US Seventh Fleet to the Taiwan Strait, increasing aid to the French in Indo-China, and speeding additional aid to the pro-American Philippine government which was battling the radical Huk insurgency. Behind those four interventions – in Korea,

China, Indo-China, and the Philippines – lay the American perception that a unified threat of formidable proportions was being mounted against Western interests by a hostile and newly aggressive world communist movement under the leadership of the Soviet Union and its Chinese junior partner.

The impact of the Korean War on the Cold War is difficult to overstate. Not only did the Korean fighting lead to an intensification and geographical expansion of the Cold War, threaten a wider conflict between the United States and the communist powers, and foster increased East–West hostility, but it also spurred a huge increase in American defence spending and, more broadly, a militarization and globalization of American foreign policy. Beyond Asia, the conflict in Korea also hastened the strengthening of NATO, the arming of Germany, and the stationing of US troops on European soil. 'It was the Korean War and not World War II that made the United States a world military-political power', diplomat Charles Bohlen has argued. With uncommon unanimity, scholars have affirmed that judgement, identifying the Korean War as a key turning point in the international history of the postwar era. America's 'real commitment to contain communism everywhere originated in the events surrounding the Korean War', contends John Lewis Gaddis. Warren I. Cohen calls it 'a war that would alter the nature of the Soviet-American confrontation, change it from a systemic political competition into an ideologically driven, militarized contest that threatened the very survival of the globe'.

Yet, as Cohen also notes, 'that a civil war in Korea would provide the critical turning point in the postwar Soviet-American relationship, and raise the possibility of world war, seems, in retrospect, nothing short of bizarre'. Certainly, in the aftermath of World War II, few places appeared less likely to emerge as a focal point of great power competition. Occupied and ruled by Japan as a colony ever since 1910, Korea factored into wartime councils merely as yet another minor and obscure territory whose future disposition fell on the

Allies' already overburdened shoulders. At the Potsdam Conference, the Americans and Soviets agreed to share occupation responsibilities there by temporarily dividing the country at the 38th parallel; they also agreed to work towards the establishment of an independent, unified Korea at the earliest practicable time. In December 1945, at a foreign ministers' meeting in Moscow, the Soviets accepted a US proposal for the establishment of a joint Soviet-American commission to prepare for the election of a provisional Korean government as a first step toward full independence. But that plan soon fell victim to larger Cold War tensions that militated against any meaningful cooperation, or compromise, between Moscow and Washington. By 1948, the occupation divisions had instead hardened. In the north, a pro-Soviet regime under the leadership of the former anti-Japanese fighter Kim Il-sung took on all the trappings of an independent regime. So, too, did its counterpart in the south: a pro-American regime headed by the virulently anti-communist Syngman Rhee, a Korean nationalist of long standing. Each side regularly rattled sabres at the other; neither North nor South Koreans could accept a permanent division of their homeland.

In 1948, the Truman administration, seeking to extricate itself gracefully from its Korean commitment, began withdrawing US military forces from the peninsula. American defence planners believed not only that US military personnel had become overextended worldwide, necessitating this pullback, but that Korea, in fact, possessed minimal strategic worth. The North Korean invasion two years later brought a different calculus to the fore. Although it might have lacked great intrinsic strategic value, Korea stood as a potent symbol, especially in view of America's role as midwife and protector of the Seoul regime. Further, the North Korean attack, sanctioned and backed by the Soviet Union and China, threatened America's credibility as a regional and global power every bit as much as it threatened the survival of the South Korean government. To Truman, Acheson, and other senior decision-makers, the stakes at risk in Korea appeared enormous.

Consequently, without any dissenting voices being raised, the president quickly authorized US military intervention. 'If the United Nations yields to the force of aggression', Truman declared publicly on 30 November, 'no nation will be safe or secure. If aggression is successful in Korea, we can expect it to spread throughout Asia and Europe to this hemisphere. We are fighting in Korea for our own national security and survival.'

That statement came right after the entry of Chinese Communist 'volunteer' forces into the fray, a development that changed the character of the Korean conflict – and, arguably, the Cold War as well. Truman and his military advisers grew overconfident after MacArthur turned the tide of battle in September 1950 by outflanking the North Koreans with his legendary Inchon landing. The UN forces under his command crossed into North Korean territory on 7 October; by 25 October, some advance units reached the Yalu River, along the North Korean-Chinese border. As they inched closer to Chinese territory, Mao informed Stalin that he had decided to send Chinese troops across the Yalu. 'The reason', he explained, 'is that if we allow the United States to occupy all of Korea and Korean revolutionary strength suffers a fundamental defeat, then the Americans will run more rampant to the detriment of the entire East.' Mao, too, saw broad regional and global implications in the Korean outcome. MacArthur, who had so cavalierly underestimated the Chinese military threat and whose forces were almost completely driven out of North Korea by the end of November, informed the Joint Chiefs of Staff: 'We face an entirely new war.'

The world faced an entirely new Cold War by that time as well, one whose boundaries reached well beyond Europe. The emergence of Mao's regime in China, the Sino-Soviet alliance, Soviet and Chinese support for North Korean adventurism, the intervention of US and UN forces in Korea, the subsequent entry of Chinese troops, the presence of communist elements within Southeast Asia's

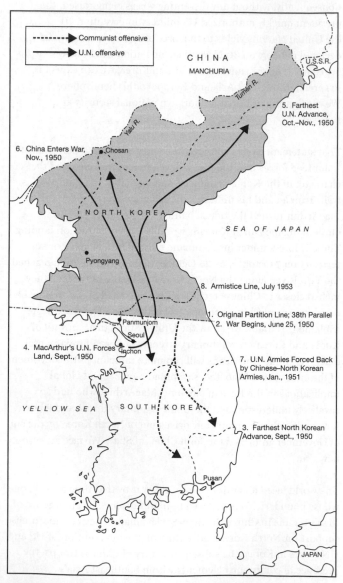

Map II. The Korean War, 1950–3.

nationalist movements – all ensured that the Cold War would remain a commanding presence in postwar Asia for a long time to come. The Korean War itself dragged on inconclusively until July 1953, when the warring parties signed an armistice that achieved little more than an exchange of prisoners-of-war and a return to the *status quo ante bellum*. The 38th parallel remained an ominous line of division – not just between North and South Korea, but between the Eastern and Western blocs.

Chapter 4
A global Cold War, 1950–8

With the Korean conflict, the Cold War became increasingly global in scope. In the decade that followed the onset of the Korean fighting, few corners of the world managed to escape the ensnaring web of superpower rivalry, competition, and conflict. Indeed, the principal international flashpoints of the 1950s and 1960s – Iran, Guatemala, Indo-China, the Taiwan Strait, Suez, Lebanon, Indonesia, Cuba, the Congo – lay well beyond the Cold War's original boundaries. Only Berlin, whose contested status triggered Soviet–American crises in 1958 and again in 1961–2, belongs to the set of immediate post-World War II disputes that precipitated the East–West breach in the first place.

The Cold War, during this period, essentially moved from the centre of the international system to its periphery. The Americans and the Soviets each identified crucial strategic, economic, and psychological interests in the developing areas of Asia, the Middle East, Latin America, and Africa, and sought to gain resources, bases, allies, and influence there. By the 1950s, those areas had emerged at the very heart of the Soviet–American struggle, a position they would retain throughout the 1960s, 1970s, and 1980s. The East–West division in Europe, by way of contrast, achieved a remarkable degree of stability; the very idea of a military conflict there became increasingly unpalatable to Soviet and American leaders, who recognized that any major confrontation in the centre would almost certainly turn nuclear. It is particularly telling that virtually all of the wars that erupted during the Cold War era were waged on Third World soil – and that all but 200,000 of the estimated 20 million people who died in wars fought between 1945 and 1990 were felled in conflicts that raged across various parts of the Third World.

Yet a fearsome nuclear armaments race between the United States and the Soviet Union also picked up steam in the Cold War's second decade, raising the spectre of a miscalculation or an uncontrollable escalation that could result in appalling devastation and the loss of untold millions of lives. These themes – the geographical expansion of the Cold War into the periphery, the achievement of relative peace and stability in Europe, and the steady build-up of nuclear arsenals on both sides – form the main emphases of this chapter.

Stabilizing East–West relations

Although the Korean War spurred the militarization and globalization of the Cold War, it also, ironically, set in motion forces that helped stabilize US–Soviet relations while institutionalizing the East–West division of Europe in a manner that decreased the likelihood of war between the superpowers. Convinced in the wake of the North Korean attack that they now faced a more aggressive and more dangerously opportunistic foe, and increasingly concerned about the vulnerability of Western Europe to a Soviet military thrust, American policy-makers redoubled their efforts to strengthen NATO. By late 1950, Truman had sent four US divisions to Europe, despite significant opposition from prominent House and Senate Republicans; begun the transformation of NATO into a real military alliance with an integrated command structure; appointed popular World War II General Dwight D. Eisenhower as NATO's first supreme commander; and initiated plans for the rearmament of Germany.

West German rearmament stood as the Truman administration's

highest priority. American strategists considered German manpower essential to the defence of Europe; they also believed that a rearmed Germany, with fully restored sovereignty, was needed in order to lock the Federal Republic into the Western orbit and to shore up the government of pro-American Chancellor Konrad Adenauer. Yet the spectre of a militarily revived Germany so soon after the demise of a regime that had brought such unparalleled horrors to Europe terrified France and other European allies. To ease their fears, the United States agreed to the concept of a European Defence Community (EDC), first advanced by the French, which proposed an intricate set of arrangements that would permit the build-up of limited West German military forces that were then to be subsumed within a broader Western European army.

The Soviets tried in vain to derail the process of German rearmament, presenting the Western allies in the spring of 1952 with a set of diplomatic notes calling for the establishment of a unified, neutralized Germany. Once again, the prospect of a resurgent Germany, its latent economic-military power co-opted by and harnessed to the West, haunted Stalin and the Soviet Politburo, prompting their effort to find a less threatening, if still risky, solution to the German problem. But Washington dismissed Moscow's demarche out of hand. A unified, neutralized Germany represented a strategic nightmare for the United States; such a state might over time tilt towards the Soviet sphere, thereby upsetting the European power balance. That was precisely what the Truman administration was determined to prevent. The Soviets soon resigned themselves to the *fait accompli* of a permanently divided Germany and took steps, in response, that resulted in their recognition of East Germany, the so-called German Democratic Republic, as a sovereign state in March 1954. Stalin and his successors recognized that the integration of a rearmed, sovereign West Germany into the US-led sphere would tip the balance of economic and military power significantly toward the West; yet they also realized that such an outcome at least carried fewer risks than that of a reunited, autonomous German state emerging once again as the balance wheel in European politics and potential future menace to Soviet security.

A surprising convergence actually developed in the thinking of Soviet and Western strategists towards the German question by the early and mid-1950s, a convergence that facilitated the stabilization of Europe and permitted a modest reduction in East–West tensions. As British Foreign Minister Selwyn Lloyd privately put it in June 1953: 'To unite Germany while Europe is divided, if practical, is fraught with danger for all. Therefore everyone – Dr. Adenauer, the Russians, the Americans, the French and ourselves – feel in our hearts that a divided Germany is safer for the time being. But none of us dare say so openly because of the effect upon German public opinion. Therefore we all publicly support a united Germany, each on his own terms.'

When the French Assembly rejected the EDC treaty in the summer of 1954, the British expeditiously devised an alternative means to accomplish the goal of a remilitarized, reintegrated West Germany. Their plan, which the Dwight D. Eisenhower administration concurred in, called for utilizing NATO as the constraining framework within which German rearmament should proceed. Later that year, during a pomp-filled conference in Paris, the NATO powers agreed to this new formula for rearming West Germany, restoring its sovereignty, and terminating the US-British-French occupation. In May 1955, a fully sovereign Federal Republic of Germany entered NATO.

Despite numerous bumps along the way, the United States achieved its core European policy objectives with the negotiation of the German contractual agreements, securing a strengthened, reinvigorated NATO in tandem with a sovereign, rearmed West Germany. It had succeeded as well in encouraging a reconciliation between Paris and Bonn and promoting a more politically integrated and economically vibrant Western Europe.

'The American design was to create a prosperous, non-Communist Europe', notes historian Melvyn P. Leffler. 'Its goal was to thwart any attempt by the Kremlin to seize Western Europe in wartime, intimidate it in peacetime, or lure West Germany into its orbit anytime.' Almost exactly ten years after the end of the war in Europe, that essential goal appeared close to realization.

In early 1953, the first leadership changes since the onset of the Cold War took place in both Washington and Moscow. But new men at the top did little to diminish the mutual mistrust and suspicion that lay at the heart of the superpower impasse. Eisenhower and his chief foreign policy adviser, Secretary of State John Foster Dulles, were, in fact, determined to prosecute the Cold War with even greater vigour than had their Democratic predecessors. The Republican Party platform of 1952, in a passage authored by Dulles, blasted the Democrats' 'tragic blunders' in foreign affairs and condemned the Truman administration's strategy of containment as a 'negative, futile, and immoral' policy that 'abandons countless human beings to a despotic and godless communism'. Not even the death of Stalin in March 1953 and the advancement of vague peace proposals from the collective leadership that had replaced the long-serving Russian dictator dented the conviction of Eisenhower and his top strategists that they faced an implacable, devious enemy. They were certain that the Soviet Union posed a military, a political, and an ideological threat of the first order; it was an adversary that appeared impervious to traditional diplomatic give-and-take and thus could only be dealt with from a position of overpowering strength. 'This is an irreconcilable conflict', Dulles told the Senate Foreign Relations Committee during his confirmation hearings. The venerable Winston Churchill, serving once again as Britain's prime minister, called for a summit meeting to test the possibility of diplomatic compromise with Moscow, but Eisenhower rejected his appeal, privately judging it a foolishly premature lurch towards appeasement.

For their part, the new Soviet rulers responded to the rearming of Germany and strengthening of NATO by consolidating their own hold over Eastern Europe. An outbreak of widespread strikes, demonstrations, and other forms of resistance to Soviet rule in East Germany in June 1953, coupled with the increasingly independent path being blazed by Yugoslavia's Joseph Broz Tito, drove home the tenuousness of Moscow's control within its own putative sphere of influence. On 14 May 1955, the Soviets formalized their security ties to their Eastern European 'allies' – the German Democratic Republic, Poland, Hungary, Czechoslovakia, Romania, Bulgaria, and Albania – with the formation of the Warsaw Pact. A loose military alliance best understood as a defensive reaction to the West's initiatives in Germany and within NATO, the Warsaw Pact symbolized the hardening of the continent's lines of division. Just one day later, the Soviets joined with the allies in signing a peace treaty with Austria which allowed for the termination of the allied occupation there in exchange for the creation of a sovereign, neutral state. Moscow also offered the West new proposals to halt the arms race, sought to reach a *modus vivendi* with Yugoslavia, and launched a series of bold diplomatic initiatives in the Third World.

Those moves, undertaken by the rambunctious but flexible Nikita S. Khrushchev, the Communist Party boss who had emerged as the dominant figure in the post-Stalinist leadership, helped facilitate the summit meeting long craved by Churchill. In July 1955, Soviet, American, British, and French heads of government met at Geneva, the first such meeting since the Potsdam Conference a decade earlier. Although no breakthroughs occurred with regard to Germany, disarmament, or any other major issues in dispute, the very fact that the conference took place seemed to herald the dawning of a more cooperative and conciliatory chapter in East–West relations. In the broadest sense, the Geneva Conference confirmed both sides' tacit recognition of the existing status quo in Europe – along with the implicit understanding that neither would risk war to overturn it. Significantly, two months after the conference closed Moscow extended diplomatic recognition to West Germany.

In a momentous speech to the Twentieth Party Congress in Moscow in February 1956, Khrushchev harshly denounced the domestic crimes and foreign policy mistakes of Stalin. The Soviet leader's secret, four-hour speech called for 'peaceful coexistence' with the capitalist powers and conceded that there were different paths towards socialism. The speech, whose contents were soon widely disseminated, shocked communists and non-communists alike. Would-be reformers in Eastern Europe were heartened by the prospect of a loosening Soviet grip. Intellectuals, students, and workers soon tested the limits of the Kremlin's tolerance for diversity and national independence. In June, labour disputes in long-restive Poland quickly turned into expressions of outright resistance to the Soviet Union. After using the Red Army to quell nationalist riots in Warsaw, Khrushchev reversed course and assented to the installation of former prime minister Wladyslaw Gomulka, a reformer who had been ousted earlier in a Stalinist purge, as the new Polish Communist Party chairman.

Similar agitation in Hungary yielded a more tragic outcome. On 23 October, student-led demonstrations throughout the country escalated into an outright insurrection against the Soviet military presence. When, at the end of the month, the reformist government of Imre Nagy announced Hungary's decision to leave the Warsaw Pact, declared itself a neutralist nation, and appealed for UN support, Khrushchev reached the limits of his tolerance for political change within Eastern Europe. To do nothing, the Soviet ruler privately ruminated, 'will give a great boost to the Americans, English, and French'. The simultaneous Anglo-French invasion of Egypt on 31 October, together with Eisenhower's re-election campaign, then entering its final days, provided the Russian leader with what he saw as a 'favourable moment' to use military force. Consequently, on 4 November,

4. Hungarians protest against the Soviet Union, November 1956.

200,000 Soviet and Warsaw Pact troops, backed by 5,500 tanks, moved to suppress the Hungarian rebels with overwhelming force. The unequal clash that ensued claimed approximately 20,000 Hungarian and as many as 3,000 Soviet lives. By 8 November, the rebellion had been crushed. The Eisenhower administration, whose pro-liberation rhetoric and provocative Radio Free Europe broadcasts had done much to encourage the anti-Soviet resistance, could do little but wring its hands about Russian brutality. Plainly, the Americans were no more willing to tempt a global conflagration over events in the Soviet sphere of influence than the Soviets would have been in response to developments in Western Europe. By the mid-1950s, a form of great power order was emerging in Europe; a few scholars have, in fact, employed the term 'Long Peace' to characterize post-World War II Europe. For some, though, as Hungarians painfully learned, that order came at a very high price.

Turmoil in the Third World

For several reasons, the developing nations of the Third World, most just emerging from decades, if not centuries, of Western colonial rule, became a focal point of Soviet–American competition during the 1950s. US national security planners recognized that the resources and markets of Third World areas were essential to the health of the world capitalist economy, the economic recoveries of Western Europe and Japan, and America's own commercial and military needs. The West, in fact, derived much of its economic-military vitality from its links to the developing world; the critical importance of Middle Eastern oil to Western Europe's peacetime needs and NATO's wartime requirements serves only as the most obvious case in point. The Soviets, especially after the death of the doctrinaire Stalin and the rise to power of the more diplomatically adroit Khrushchev, made a concerted bid for friends and allies among the Third World's uncommitted nations in order to dilute that aspect of Western strength. Utilizing diplomacy, trade, and generous development loans, the Kremlin sought to gain influence and access to resources and bases, especially among the Afro-Asian nations, while weakening the hold of the West. The Marxist-Leninist development model appealed to many Third World intellectuals and political leaders, who were impressed with the Soviet Union's leap from backwardness to the status of a military-industrial giant in a mere generation.

That fact facilitated the Kremlin's bid for friends and support, much as the taint of Western imperialism, racism, arrogance, and continuing control over indigenous resources complicated the task of American diplomats. US policy-makers became convinced during the 1950s that the outcome of the struggle over the periphery could well tip the balance of global power towards – or against – the West. The 'much enlarged' Soviet effort in the developing world, Secretary of State Dean Rusk announced to the Senate in February 1961, demonstrated that the Soviet–American struggle had shifted 'from the military problem in Western Europe to a genuine contest for the underdeveloped countries'. He warned that 'the battles for Africa, Latin America, the Middle East, [and] Asia are now joined, not on a military plain in the first instance, but for influence, prestige, loyalty, and so forth, and the stakes there are very high.'

The Iranian crisis of 1951–3 encapsulates nearly all of those larger themes. It was born of a struggle between an indigenous nationalist regime determined to regain control over its economy and a Western power unwilling to renegotiate the terms of a highly lucrative oil concession. Ardent nationalist leader Mohammed Mossadeq precipitated the crisis when he nationalized the oilfields and refineries of the Anglo-Iranian Oil Company (AIOC) in the spring of 1951. The Iranian prime minister was seeking to wrest greater profits for his nation from the vast petroleum reserves that constituted Iran's most valuable resource, a resource that had long been monopolized by the giant, British-owned AIOC. Great Britain's adamant refusal to negotiate in good faith with the

Mossadeq government and its subsequent resort to a boycott of Iranian oil produced rising tensions that soon took on strong Cold War overtones. Although sympathetic at first to what it, too, viewed as an unwelcome challenge by an upstart Third World regime to the unwritten rules that had long governed commercial arrangements between the industrialized and the less developed nations, the United States spied a much more serious threat in Iran's opportunistic neighbour to the north. The Truman administration offered its services as a mediator principally because it feared a destabilizing confrontation from which the Soviets seemed sure to benefit. The British refusal to compromise blunted American mediation efforts, however, and prompted Mossadeq both to welcome Soviet aid and to turn for internal support to the pro-Soviet Tudeh Party. In response, the Eisenhower administration launched, with the British, a covert operation that helped topple Mossadeq while restoring the pro-Western Shah of Iran, Mohammed Reza Pahlavi, to power as a royal autocrat.

Although the origins of the Anglo-Iranian dispute had nothing to do with the Cold War, it was US fears of Soviet adventurism – however exaggerated – that drove American policy. Behind its covert intervention in Iranian affairs lay the two central preoccupations of America's Middle Eastern policy during the early Cold War: a determination to contain the Soviet Union, and thus deny to it influence over the region's emerging post-colonial states, and a determination to protect Western Europe's access to vital oil supplies. 'An adequate supply of oil to Western Europe ranks almost equal in priority with an adequate supply for ourselves', Eisenhower remarked to an adviser after Mossadeq's fall from power. 'The West must, for self-preservation, retain access to Mid-East oil.'

A second dispute with heavy neo-colonial overtones, that between Britain and Egypt over who would control the mammoth Cairo-Suez military complex, also bedevilled American efforts to forge a stable, pro-Western Middle East. It led indirectly to the most serious international incident of the decade, the Suez Crisis of 1956. The roots of that crisis lay in Egypt's refusal to enlist in any of the anti-Soviet defence organizations that the Americans and British sought to assemble in the early and mid-1950s. The bitterness engendered by the dispute with London disinclined the Egyptians to cooperate with a West they associated with continuing imperial machinations. With Egypt and most other leading Arab states refusing to enter into a collective security agreement with the Western powers, the Americans and British gravitated towards the alternative 'northern tier' concept. In February 1955, consequently, Britain, Turkey, Pakistan, Iran, and Iraq signed the Baghdad Pact, a loose mutual security agreement intended to extend the containment shield to the Middle East. Although American pressure, along with promises of military and economic largesse, were instrumental in the negotiations leading to the agreement, Washington chose not to participate directly so as to avoid unduly alienating Arab states with whom it was still cultivating friendly relations.

Yet that initiative actually spurred the very regional instability it aimed to quell. The creation of the Baghdad Pact struck Egypt's nationalist strongman Gamal Abdel Nasser as an act of open hostility since conservative Iraq, the pact's sole Arab signatory, was Egypt's traditional rival within the Arab world. In the autumn of 1955, Nasser signed an arms deal with Czechoslovakia in order to counter an Iraq now bolstered militarily by its formal association with the Western-sponsored Baghdad grouping. Alarmed by Egypt's seeming drift towards the Soviet camp, the Eisenhower administration, in December 1955, offered a carrot: generous funding for the Aswan Dam project, the centrepiece of Egypt's ambitious development plans. But Egypt's support for commando raids into Israel, its continuing neutralist line in foreign policy, and its recognition of the People's Republic of China in May 1956 aroused American ire. On 19 July 1956, Secretary of State Dulles abruptly announced that the United States was rescinding its Aswan Dam financing offer. 'May you choke to death on your fury', a

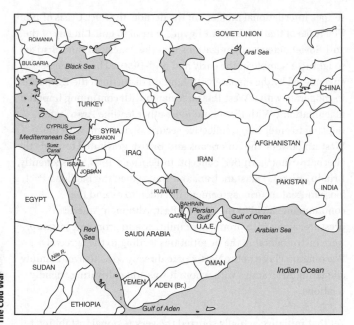

Map III. The Middle East 1956.

defiant Nasser railed at the United States. World Bank President
Eugene Black warned Dulles that 'all hell might break loose'.

On 26 July, Nasser proved Black prescient. In a bold and wholly
unanticipated move, he nationalized the Suez Canal Company, an
Anglo-French concern, vowing to operate the vital international
waterway efficiently and to use the revenues it generated to finance
his high-priority dam project. After desultory negotiations, in which
Dulles laboured assiduously to find an alternative to open conflict,
collusion between Britain, France, and Israel led to their joint
military action against Egypt in late October 1956. To the shock and
dismay of its allies, the United States forcefully condemned their
invasion, terming it a blatant and unjustified act of military
aggression that violated the rule of law. When, on 5 November, the

Soviets denounced the attack on Egypt and bumptiously threatened retaliation against Britain and France if they did not immediately cease their aggression, the Suez crisis suddenly metamorphosed into a potentially grave East–West confrontation. Persistent US pressure on its allies helped to produce a cease-fire, thereby defusing the danger posed by what the Americans judged to be an empty, but still disturbing, Soviet bluff.

In the aftermath of the Suez crisis, the United States assumed even greater responsibilities in the Middle East. Eisenhower's greatest fear was that the Soviet Union would move into the vacuum created by the waning of British and French power in the region. As he told a group of Congressmen on 1 January 1957: 'The existing vacuum in the Middle East must be filled by the United States before it is filled by Russia.' The so-called Eisenhower Doctrine, which the president proposed to Congress on 5 January, created a special fund to provide economic and military assistance to pro-Western regimes in the Middle East. It also threatened the use of military force, if necessary, to stop 'overt armed aggression from any nation controlled by International Communism'. The vague doctrine certainly made manifest the deepening American commitment to a region that US strategists now imagined on the front lines of the Cold War. It also provided the pretext for Eisenhower's dispatch of US forces to Lebanon the following year, after a bloody coup in Iraq toppled the pro-Western monarchy there and called into question US credibility within the region. Yet the deepest sources of regional instability – the Arab–Israeli dispute, deep-seated resentment among Arabs at the legacies of Western imperialism, and the appeal of radical, pan-Arab nationalism – remained impervious to US troop deployments, economic enticements, diplomatic schemes, and mediation proposals.

Southeast Asia emerged at this time as another region of intense Cold War contestation. American policy-makers worried that the unsettled conditions prevailing in an area beset by enormous economic difficulties, a tenuous and incomplete transition from colonialism to independence, and still-raging colonial conflicts in Indo-China and Malaya made all of Southeast Asia ripe for communist penetration. The stakes struck US analysts as alarmingly high. Declared Charles Bohlen, one of the State Department's top Soviet specialists: the 'loss of Southeast Asia' to communism would exert so profound an impact on the overall balance of power that, if it occurred, 'we would have lost the Cold War'. In mid-1952, Secretary of State Acheson struck a similar note, exclaiming to British Foreign Minister Anthony Eden that 'we are lost if we lose southeast Asia without a fight' and hence 'we must do what we can to save Southeast Asia'.

If the prospect of the Soviet Union exploiting regional ferment to gain a foothold in the Middle East proved the foremost American fear in that region, the prospect of China employing outright military aggression to achieve expansionist ends ranked as the predominant American fear in Southeast Asia. In a policy paper approved by Truman in June 1952, the National Security Council spelled out Washington's over-riding concern. The defection of any single Southeast Asia country to the Sino-Soviet bloc, it warned, 'would have critical psychological, political and economic consequences', and 'would probably lead to relatively swift submission to or an alignment with communism by the remaining countries of the group'. In short, a domino effect could be expected in which communist control over one country would, without prompt and vigorous counteraction, lead to communist control over the entire region – and possibly well beyond. Such an eventuality would exert highly detrimental economic effects on both Western Europe and Japan, deny critical strategic resources to the West, strike a blow at the credibility and prestige of the United States as a world power, and lend weight to the notion that the momentum of history lay with communism and not with the Western democracies.

Indo-China, where the communist-led Viet Minh insurgents had, since 1946, been thwarting all French attempts to suppress them, thanks in part to invaluable Chinese military and logistical support, appeared the most likely place for a communist breakthrough. It served as the focal point, accordingly, of America's containment efforts in Southeast Asia. Beginning just prior to the Korean War and increasing progressively over the next few years, US military aid essentially underwrote the French war effort. By early 1954, however, the French people and government had grown weary of a conflict that had proven costly, protracted, and deeply unpopular. Rejecting American counsel, they sought a graceful diplomatic exit. A great power conference on Indo-China, consequently, convened at Geneva in May 1954. It was followed quickly by a decisive Viet Minh triumph over the embattled French garrison at Dienbienphu in remote, northwestern Vietnam. Together those developments hastened the end of French rule in Indo-China. Unable to win at the conference table what had been lost on the battlefield, the Western powers accepted the temporary division of Vietnam at the 17th parallel, awarding the northern half of the country to Ho's Viet Minh. The Vietnamese leader's Soviet and Chinese allies pressed him to settle for the proverbial half a loaf, to his great frustration, because they wanted to avoid provoking the Americans and risking another military confrontation with the West so soon after the Korean cease-fire.

For its part, the Eisenhower administration sought to salvage what it could from an outcome that represented not just a humiliating national defeat for France but a global, Cold War setback for the United States. In an effort to draw the line against further communist advances in Southeast Asia, the Americans took the lead in forming the Southeast Asia Treaty Organization (SEATO) in September 1954. It brought together the United States, France, Great Britain, Australia, New Zealand, the Philippines, Thailand, and Pakistan in a loose, and rather toothless, anti-communist alliance intended to signal resolve to the Chinese and Soviets. Eisenhower, Dulles, and their associates also moved immediately to supplant French influence with American in South Vietnam, pouring US dollars, advisers, and materiel into the fledgling

Republic of Vietnam in order to prevent its being absorbed by North Vietnam, either through force of arms or via the ballot box. Certain that the all-Vietnam elections scheduled for 1956 would result in a resounding victory for Ho Chi Minh, pro-American Premier Ngo Dinh Diem cancelled them. Vietnam thus joined Germany and Korea as another nation divided by Cold War tensions that made unification too risky.

In the Middle East, in Southeast Asia, and throughout the Third World, the United States turned with increasing frequency to covert operations during the 1950s to achieve its foreign policy objectives. Indeed, the CIA became a favoured Cold War instrument for American policy-makers since it promised efficient, cost-effective actions that precluded the need for conventional armed forces and could plausibly be denied if the veil of secrecy were breached. Between 1949 and 1952, the number of CIA personnel grew exponentially, along with the agency's budget, and the number of overseas CIA stations expanded from 7 to 47. In 1953, as already noted, the CIA played an instrumental role in the overthrow of Iran's Mossadeq. The next year, it played an equally instrumental role in the ouster of Guatemala's leftist leader Jacobo Arbenz Guzman. The latter's nationalization of the US-owned United Fruit Company, together with his tolerance for Guatemala's tiny communist party, labelled him, in US eyes, as a dangerous extremist who might give the Soviet Union the opening it needed to establish a Western hemisphere foothold. Although American assessments of both Mossadeq and Arbenz as proto-communists were way off base, as the bulk of recent scholarship has demonstrated conclusively, the interventions in Iran and Guatemala demonstrate the depth of US fears about the direction of political change in the Third World. The CIA's successes in Iran and Guatemala shrouded the agency in an aura of mysterious near-invincibility, and probably encouraged Eisenhower and his successors to employ covert means in an oft-times counterproductive manner. Covert intervention against an anti-Western regime in Syria backfired in 1957, for example, as did a wildly reckless paramilitary effort to unseat Indonesia's Sukarno

5. Ho Chi Minh, president of the Democratic Republic of Vietnam.

the following year. Both were exposed, and did more harm than good to the American cause. The growing addiction to covert action proved difficult to break, however. It derived partly from the lure of easy, cost-efficient success – from the same budgetary pressures, in fact, that made the United States so reliant on nuclear weapons to achieve foreign policy goals.

The arms race

Both the United States and the Soviet Union inaugurated major arms build-ups – conventional and nuclear – following the outbreak of the Korean War. Between 1950 and 1953, the United States increased its armed forces by over a million troops while also significantly expanding its production of aircraft, naval vessels, armoured vehicles, and other instruments of conventional warfare. Its nuclear build-up was even more impressive. In October 1952, the Americans successfully tested a thermonuclear device, or H-bomb, that was exponentially more powerful than those used over Hiroshima and Nagasaki. In October 1954, they successfully detonated an even more potent one. Delivery systems kept pace. Through the end of the 1950s, the American nuclear deterrent depended upon medium-range bombers that could strike Soviet territory in two-way missions only from forward bases in Europe. But by the decade's close, the United States had enhanced its nuclear striking power with the deployment of some 538 B-52 intercontinental bombers, each capable of striking Soviet targets from bases in the United States. In 1955, Eisenhower also ordered the development of intercontinental ballistic missiles (ICBMs) that would permit nuclear warheads to be launched against the Soviet Union from American soil. By 1960, the United States began deploying its first generation of ICBMs, along with its first batch of submarine-based ballistic missiles.

Those deployments gave the United States the coveted 'triad' of bomber-, land-, and submarine-based nuclear weapons, each part of the triad capable of obliterating major Soviet targets. The total

US nuclear arsenal had grown from approximately 1,000 warheads in 1953, Eisenhower's first year in office, to 18,000 in 1960, his last. By then, the US Strategic Air Command (SAC) boasted a total of 1,735 strategic bombers capable of dropping nuclear weapons on Soviet targets.

The Soviet Union laboured to keep pace. Between 1950 and 1955, the Red Army expanded by 3 million troops to create an armed force of nearly 5.8 million – before Khrushchev ordered force cuts in the mid-1950s to reduce Moscow's exorbitant defence budget. But the Soviet Union's marked edge over the United States and NATO in men under arms was paralleled, and vitiated, by a significant inferiority in virtually every other measure of military strength. That disparity was particularly glaring in the nuclear sphere. The Soviets successfully tested their first thermonuclear device in August 1953, and a more powerful one in November 1955. Their delivery capability remained severely limited, however. Before 1955, the Soviets remained incapable of carrying out a nuclear strike against the United States and, consequently, relied for deterrent purposes on the ability of their bombers to hit Western European targets. By the end of the decade, the Soviet strategic bomber fleet still could only reach the continental United States on one-way bombing missions from Arctic bases, missions that would have been highly vulnerable to US interceptors. Not until the early 1960s did the Soviet Union begin to produce and deploy ICBMs and, despite the much-ballyhooed launch of Sputnik, the first earth-orbiting satellite, in 1957, the Soviet Union lagged behind the United States in all significant measures of technological prowess as well. It is telling that Eisenhower, following an NSC discussion in 1953 of the comparative nuclear capabilities of the two superpowers, remarked about his Soviet counterparts: 'They must be scared as hell.'

Yet, paradoxically, in the late 1950s certain quarters within the United States began criticizing Eisenhower for allowing a 'missile gap' to open between the Americans and the Soviets. The criticisms derived from the fear that Moscow's first successful test of an ICBM

A global Cold War, 1950–8

in August 1957 and the launch of its Sputnik satellite two months later together signified a dramatic assault on America's vaunted technological superiority. Not only had the Russians seemingly beaten the Americans into space, but Khrushchev's penchant for boasting and blustering about the number of long-range missiles his nation was developing led even some sober-minded strategic analysts to worry about a Soviet military-technological surge. More than a few fretted that the balance of power might be shifting from West to East, a trend some suspected was abetted by the softness of American society and the declining aptitude for mathematics and science among US schoolchildren. Eisenhower remained unruffled. Aided by secret reconnaissance photographs produced by covert overflights of Soviet territory, he knew that such was not the case; that the United States maintained a formidable lead over its rival in deliverable nuclear weapons. Still, a political frenzy surrounded the supposed missile gap, and the non-existent gap actually emerged as a galvanizing issue in the 1960 presidential election.

Arms races have characterized international rivalries throughout recorded history. What makes that of the Cold War era unique is, of course, the nuclear dimension. Scholars, policy analysts, and governmental strategists have long ruminated about how the availability of weapons capable of wreaking unparalleled destruction shaped the contours and course of the Cold War. The question is as critically important as it is difficult to answer with any degree of precision. On the one hand, nuclear weapons probably lent a degree of stability to the superpower relationship, and almost certainly diminished the likelihood of open hostilities in Europe. NATO's essential strategy for repelling a Soviet conventional invasion pivoted on the recognition that any European war would be a nuclear war; powerful incentives thus existed on both sides to avoid a conflict that would inevitably cause enormous losses of life for attackers and defenders alike. At an NSC meeting in January 1956, Eisenhower sagely emphasized what he called the 'transcendent consideration' in all debates over nuclear strategy – 'namely that nobody can win in a thermonuclear war'.

On the other hand, Eisenhower also accepted as official doctrine during his first year in the White House that 'in the event of hostilities, the United States will consider nuclear weapons to be as available for us as other munitions'. His administration sanctioned the introduction of the first battlefield nuclear weapons into Germany in November 1953, presided over the enormous nuclear weapons and delivery systems build-up detailed above, promoted 'massive retaliation' as a core principle of the US defence posture, and threatened the use of nuclear weapons during the final stage of the Korean War and in an effort to deter Beijing during the Taiwan Strait crisis of 1954–5.

Americans exhibited, in short, a somewhat contradictory attitude towards nuclear weapons and their value in achieving national security ends during the first decade and a half of the atomic era. While privately and publicly decrying the folly of nuclear conflict that no side could win, they simultaneously strove mightily to achieve a clear superiority in nuclear arms. The fact of American nuclear superiority almost certainly encouraged US risk-taking in later crises over Taiwan, Berlin, and Cuba, as the next chapter will show, and thus helped to exacerbate an already perilous phase of the Cold War.

Chapter 5
From confrontation to detente, 1958–68

In the late 1950s, the Cold War entered perhaps its most dangerous phase, the time in which the danger of general nuclear war was highest. A succession of crises, culminating in 1962 with the epochal confrontation between Washington and Moscow over the presence of Soviet missiles in Cuba, brought the world perilously close to a nuclear conflagration. On both sides of the superpower divide, risk-taking and shrill rhetoric reached levels not witnessed since the late 1940s.

Soviet Premier Khrushchev chilled American observers with his boasts about Soviet economic and technological prowess and his infamous remark that the Soviet Union would soon be turning out missiles like sausages. In January 1961, he vowed to lend Moscow's active support to wars of national liberation – wars that he said 'will continue as long as imperialism exists, as long as colonialism exists'. The communist world was destined to bury the West, the Russian ruler was fond of saying.

Not to be outdone, newly elected President John F. Kennedy implored Congress in his first state-of-the-union message that same month to provide sufficient funds for 'a Free World force so powerful as to make any aggression clearly futile'. Neither the Soviet Union nor China, he said, 'has yielded its ambitions for world domination'. The young chief executive offered a bleak vision of the global situation, noting that he spoke 'in an hour of national peril' and declaring it 'by no means certain' that the nation would endure. 'Each day the crises multiply', Kennedy stressed, 'Each day their solution grows more difficult. Each day we draw nearer the hour of maximum danger, as weapons spread and hostile forces grow stronger.'

This chapter explores the events and forces that made the late 1950s and early 1960s a period of seemingly perpetual crisis. It also examines the partial rapprochement between Washington and Moscow that began in 1963 and the deepening US involvement in Vietnam which threatened to derail that rapprochement.

Years of 'maximum danger', 1958–62

The years from 1958 to 1962 brought an unprecedented string of East–West confrontations, several of which involved nuclear brinkmanship. In 1958 alone, there was covert US intervention in Indonesia, a bloody coup that toppled the pro-Western government of Iraq, the subsequent dispatch of US marines to Lebanon, and a series of high-stakes showdowns between Washington and Beijing over Taiwan and between Washington and Moscow over Berlin.

On 17 July 1958, just two days after US Marines landed in Lebanon, Mao Zedong authorized preparations for a confrontation with the United States in the Taiwan Strait. He aimed to 'pin down the US imperialists [and] prove China supports the national liberation movements in the Middle East with not only words but also deeds'. Such boldness, the Chinese leader believed, would mock Khrushchev's contemptible moderation and thus gain for Beijing a leadership role among Third World revolutionary forces, while also helping to mobilize the Chinese people behind his radical domestic policies. On 23 August, Mao's forces began shelling the off-shore islands of Quemoy and Matsu, islands claimed and defended by

Chiang Kai-shek's Chinese nationalist forces. Eisenhower and Dulles immediately suspected, as they had in the earlier 1954–5 crisis, that the artillery barrage might be a prelude to a full-scale invasion of Taiwan, which the United States was pledged by treaty to defend. In response, Eisenhower put the US military on full alert, rushed a formidable naval armada to the Taiwan Strait, and authorized the dispatch of additional nuclear-equipped forces to the region. He was striving, essentially, to deter Chinese aggression with a show of overwhelming force combined with unmistakable public declarations of resolve.

In early September, Khrushchev sent his foreign minister, Andrei Gromyko, to Beijing in an effort to defuse the crisis. The Russian visitor was 'flabbergasted' to hear repeated expressions of Chinese bravado; his hosts informed him at one point that while they recognized their actions would likely lead to a 'local war' with the United States, they were 'ready to take all the hard blows, including atomic bombs and the destruction of [their] cities'. The United States was, in fact, readying a nuclear response. Eisenhower's military advisers urged the use of low-yield nuclear bombs against Chinese military installations, action, they acknowledged, that would cause millions of civilian casualties. Khrushchev upped the ante with a menacing letter to the American president on 19 September, in which he emphasized that Moscow, too, 'has atomic and hydrogen weapons'. Should the United States use such weapons against China, he warned, it 'would spark off a conflagration of a world war' and thus 'doom to certain death sons of the American people'.

The crisis eased when, on 6 October, Mao unilaterally announced that he was ceasing the shelling of Quemoy and Matsu for one week, provided that the United States end its convoys in the Taiwan Strait. Although it ended with a whimper rather than a big bang, the episode illuminates several important themes about this unusually tense juncture of the Cold War. First, Mao knowingly courted a military confrontation with the United States that could easily have triggered devastating nuclear strikes against the Chinese mainland. His rashness in so doing points to the dangerously unpredictable role of China in Cold War politics. Second, the Taiwan Strait standoff demonstrates the willingness of the United States to again cross the nuclear threshold – even over a decidedly non-vital piece of real estate. The Eisenhower administration saw Mao's gamble as a serious test of US credibility, and hence one that demanded a firm response; since Taiwan could not be defended with conventional forces alone, nuclear weapons and the threat to use them served as the only means of deterrence. Had Mao not backed off – had he actually called the American bluff – there is no reason to believe that Eisenhower would not have authorized the use of nuclear weapons against China. Finally, the crisis underscores the significance of mounting Sino-Soviet tensions to the larger Cold War dynamic. Mistrust and competition between the two communist giants, each determined to prove its toughness and ideological purity in a bid for leadership of the communist world, formed an increasingly destabilizing factor in international affairs.

Khrushchev initiated the next major Cold War crisis, in part to counter charges that the Soviets had grown weak and vacillating *vis-à-vis* the West. The Soviet leader, in his own fashion as compulsive a risk-taker as Mao, chose Berlin to make his move. On 10 November 1958, he suddenly announced Moscow's intention to sign a new treaty with East Germany that would supersede the World War II agreements that had sanctioned the anomalous, joint occupation of the former German capital that still obtained. In a subsequent declaration, Khrushchev stated that Berlin must be transformed into a demilitarized, 'free city', and he gave the Western powers just six months, until 27 May 1959, to negotiate directly with the German Democratic Republic if they wanted to maintain their presence within and transit rights to and from Berlin. The Soviet ruler, calculating that Washington would be strongly disinclined to risk war over a city more than a hundred miles from the West German border, believed that he could reassert the vigour and boldness of Soviet foreign policy. He aimed as well to shore up a troubled East German client state that was haemorrhaging population to West Germany via Berlin's open borders. In characteristically blustering style, Khrushchev had Foreign Minister Gromyko deliver a note to the United States which taunted that only 'madmen can go the length of unleashing another war over the preservation of privileges of occupiers in West Berlin'.

The Soviet challenge hit the West at its most exposed and vulnerable flank. The United States and its chief NATO partners were agreed that to relinquish their rights in Berlin, or to lend legitimacy to the East German regime by negotiating directly with it, would be to strike a dagger into Adenauer's West Germany, which continued to exalt the goal of German unification. Yet, as the Soviets also doubtless appreciated, talk of war over an isolated, indefensible Western outpost smack in the middle of the Soviet sphere of influence would inevitably sow dissension within Western ranks. Indeed, British Prime Minister Harold Macmillan candidly informed US officials that the British 'were not prepared to face obliteration for the sake of two million Berlin Germans, their former enemies'. Believing its own credibility as well as the viability of the Western alliance to be on the line, the Eisenhower administration once again chose to hold firm – once again, at the risk of escalation all the way to nuclear war. Eisenhower, Dulles, and the Joint Chiefs of Staff were well aware that West Berlin could not be defended by conventional military means; in view of the city's weighty symbolic importance, they were prepared to use nuclear weapons to defend Western rights there.

Khrushchev allowed the 27 May deadline to lapse when he recognized America's unyielding determination to maintain the status quo, even at the risk of hostilities. Shifting course, the Russian strongman proposed a four-power foreign ministers' meeting to discuss Berlin and other matters separating East and West, with the prospect of a head-of-government summit meeting to follow. It bears emphasizing that the overwhelming superiority of the American nuclear arsenal seems to have emboldened the Americans in both the Berlin and Taiwan Strait crises of the late 1950s and, once push came to shove, compelled the Soviets to back down in the face of US nuclear brinkmanship.

At Eisenhower's invitation, Khrushchev visited the United States in the autumn of 1959, ushering in a temporary thaw in Soviet American relations dubbed by journalists the 'Spirit of Camp David'. The two leaders could not resolve the Berlin impasse, but they did agree to attend a summit meeting at Paris the following spring. Just prior to the opening of the Paris gathering, however, Soviet–American relations were dealt a severe blow when the Russians shot down a high-flying American U-2 spy plane over the Urals. The U-2 reconnaissance flights, which the United States had been conducting ever since 1956, gave Eisenhower crucial intelligence about the Soviet missile programme – and its limitations. Instead of downplaying the affair, Khrushchev chose to exploit it for maximum propaganda purposes, theatrically producing Francis Gary Powers, the American pilot, to embarrass Eisenhower after the latter had denied publicly that the flight took place. Khrushchev then walked out of the Paris summit before the formal sessions had even begun. As Eisenhower's tenure in office came to a close, relations between Washington and Moscow were more frigid than they had been at his first inauguration eight years earlier. They would soon grow even worse.

In June 1961, Khrushchev rekindled the flames of the simmering Berlin crisis during a tense meeting with new president John F. Kennedy at Vienna. The impetuous Soviet leader served notice on Kennedy that he intended to sign a separate peace treaty with East Germany within six months if there was no change in Berlin's status. He blustered that if the United States wanted to go to war over Berlin, 'there was nothing the USSR could do about it. . . . History will be the judge of our actions'. Rattled by Khrushchev's threatening tone, the untested American leader believed his

6. Kennedy and Khrushchev greet each other at the start of the Vienna summit of June 1961.

nation's and his own personal credibility were under direct challenge. JFK reasoned that a display of toughness constituted the only practicable course of action; to back down would just be to invite aggression elsewhere. 'We cannot and will not permit the Communists to drive us out of Berlin', he vowed in a 25 July speech, 'either gradually or by force'. To add muscle to his defiant public rhetoric, the president asked Congress for a $3.2 billion supplement to the defence budget, authority to call up military reservists, and an additional $207 million to initiate a fallout shelter programme to prepare the American people for a future nuclear attack.

Behind Khrushchev's belligerent challenge to the West lay a ticking time bomb for the Soviet bloc: the alarming rate of East German defections. Between 1949 and mid-1961, approximately 2.7 million East Germans fled to the West – equivalent to the entire population of the Republic of Ireland – most of them utilizing the Berlin escape hatch. That embarrassing problem gravely undermined the viability of Moscow's East German client state and its hard-line leader, Walter Ulbricht. As the defections daily grew more numerous through the mid-summer of 1961, the East Germans suddenly began to construct a barbed wire barrier to separate the Soviet sector of the former German capital from the Western sectors. The temporary barrier of 13 August soon became a permanent wall, replete with armed guards, an ugly and ominous symbol of Europe's division into Western and communist blocs. War was averted, to be sure, and Khrushchev was able to provide a form of life-support to the German Democratic Republic, but those achievements came at a high political and propaganda cost for the Soviet Union and East Germany. 'It's not a very nice solution', mused a pragmatic Kennedy, 'but a wall is a hell of a lot better than a war'. Fortunately for the American president, he never had to confront the fundamental question of whether Berlin was worth a war that would almost certainly have claimed tens of millions of lives.

Other international flashpoints also competed for the attention of policy-makers in Moscow and Washington during this crisis-filled period, many emanating from the ever-turbulent Third World. Although the end of empire in Africa proceeded relatively smoothly, with 16 nations acquiring independence in 1960 alone, the messy denouement of Belgian rule in the Congo that year generated yet another full-blown superpower confrontation. When the Soviets dispatched military equipment and technicians to support the fledgling regime of Patrice Lumumba, the Americans dispatched an assassination team in an unsuccessful attempt to dispose of the embattled Lumumba, an ardent nationalist whom they wrongly tagged as a wild-eyed radical and Russian stalking horse. In 1961, pro-American Congolese forces murdered Lumumba, accomplishing what the CIA itself had failed to do; at the same time, Joseph Mobuto, America's favoured candidate, emerged as the dominant figure in a new Congo government. The United States thus managed temporarily to thwart Soviet ambitions in central Africa, if at the cost of imposing Cold

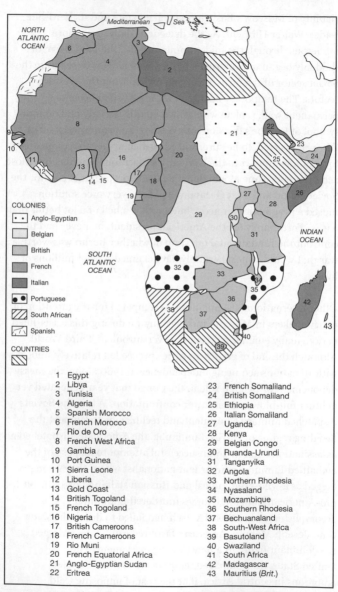

COLONIES

· · · Anglo-Egyptian
　　 Belgian
　　 British
　　 French
　　 Italian
● ● Portuguese
▨ ▨ South African
╱ ╱ Spanish

COUNTRIES
▨

1	Egypt
2	Libya
3	Tunisia
4	Algeria
5	Spanish Morocco
6	French Morocco
7	Rio de Oro
8	French West Africa
9	Gambia
10	Port Guinea
11	Sierra Leone
12	Liberia
13	Gold Coast
14	British Togoland
15	French Togoland
16	Nigeria
17	British Cameroons
18	French Cameroons
19	Rio Muni
20	French Equatorial Africa
21	Anglo-Egyptian Sudan
22	Eritrea
23	French Somaliland
24	British Somaliland
25	Ethiopia
26	Italian Somaliland
27	Uganda
28	Kenya
29	Belgian Congo
30	Ruanda-Urundi
31	Tanganyika
32	Angola
33	Northern Rhodesia
34	Nyasaland
35	Mozambique
36	Southern Rhodesia
37	Bechuanaland
38	South-West Africa
39	Basutoland
40	Swaziland
41	South Africa
42	Madagascar
43	Mauritius (*Brit.*)

Map IV. Africa in 1945.

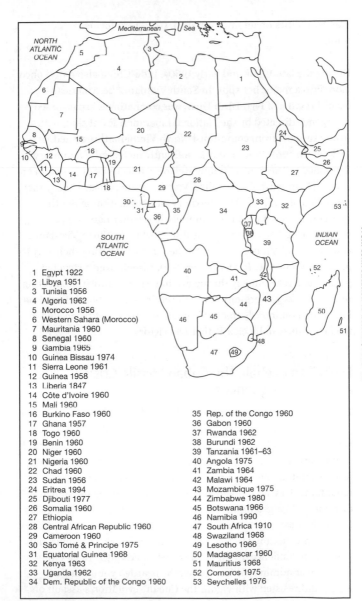

1 Egypt 1922
2 Libya 1951
3 Tunisia 1956
4 Algeria 1962
5 Morocco 1956
6 Western Sahara (Morocco)
7 Mauritania 1960
8 Senegal 1960
9 Gambia 1965
10 Guinea Bissau 1974
11 Sierra Leone 1961
12 Guinea 1958
13 Liberia 1847
14 Côte d'Ivoire 1960
15 Mali 1960
16 Burkino Faso 1960
17 Ghana 1957
18 Togo 1960
19 Benin 1960
20 Niger 1960
21 Nigeria 1960
22 Chad 1960
23 Sudan 1956
24 Eritrea 1994
25 Djibouti 1977
26 Somalia 1960
27 Ethiopia
28 Central African Republic 1960
29 Cameroon 1960
30 São Tomé & Principe 1975
31 Equatorial Guinea 1968
32 Kenya 1963
33 Uganda 1962
34 Dem. Republic of the Congo 1960
35 Rep. of the Congo 1960
36 Gabon 1960
37 Rwanda 1962
38 Burundi 1962
39 Tanzania 1961–63
40 Angola 1975
41 Zambia 1964
42 Malawi 1964
43 Mozambique 1975
44 Zimbabwe 1980
45 Botswana 1966
46 Namibia 1990
47 South Africa 1910
48 Swaziland 1968
49 Lesotho 1966
50 Madagascar 1960
51 Mauritius 1968
52 Comoros 1975
53 Seychelles 1976

Map V. Africa in 2000 (with dates of Independence).

War geopolitics on an impoverished, strife-torn former
colony.

During the late 1950s and early 1960s, Indo-China also flared once
more into a major hot spot. In South Vietnam, the American-
backed regime of Ngo Dinh Diem was combating a broad-based
insurgency directed by the National Liberation Front that, with
strong support from communist North Vietnam, threatened its
survival. In 1961–2, Kennedy significantly increased US military
assistance to Diem, dispatching well over 10,000 US advisers in an
effort to help crush the so-called 'Viet Cong' guerrillas, who, by then,
controlled about half of the territory and population of South
Vietnam. Meanwhile, the communist-led Pathet Lao in
neighbouring Laos, with logistical support from North Vietnam
and the Soviet Union, seemed on the verge of shooting their way to
power in Vientiane. In December 1960, Eisenhower instructed
president-elect Kennedy during a White House transition meeting
that Laos was 'the present key to the entire area of South East Asia'.
He warned ominously that US combat troops might be needed in
the near future to block a Pathet Lao victory.

Eyeball to eyeball: the Cuban Missile Crisis and its consequences

But the most worrisome area of all for the United States at this time
proved the island-nation of Cuba, lying just 90 miles off the
southern tip of Florida. A home-grown revolutionary, the fiery and
charismatic Fidel Castro, had fought his way to power in Havana
from his initial guerrilla base in the rugged Sierra Maestra
mountains. Having toppled and forced into exile the unpopular
dictator and longstanding US ally Fulgencio Batista by New Year's
Day 1959, Castro immediately launched an ambitious revolutionary
programme designed to free Cuba from its historic economic and
political dependence on the United States. From the outset, the
Eisenhower administration viewed the bearded young radical
warily and resisted with vigour the Cuban revolution's assault on

US property interests. Partly to counter US hostility, and partly because of his own ideological affinities, Castro turned to the Soviet Union, welcoming its diplomatic and economic support. Khrushchev, for his part, leaped at what appeared a windfall opportunity to challenge his principal rival in its own backyard. In the summer of 1960, following the establishment of close diplomatic and trade links between Havana and Moscow, the Eisenhower administration imposed a trade embargo on Cuba, suspended Cuban sugar's favoured access to the US market, and hatched plots through the CIA to assassinate Castro. Eisenhower also approved the arming and training of a group of Cuban exiles for possible use as a future invasion force.

During the 1960 presidential campaign, Kennedy hammered away persistently at the Cuba problem. He called Castro a 'source of maximum danger' and excoriated Eisenhower and Vice President Richard M. Nixon, the latter his principal opponent, for permitting a 'communist satellite' to spring up on 'our very doorstep'. Following Kennedy's victory in the November election, Eisenhower encouraged JFK to expand the exile programme. In retaliation for the Castro regime's nationalization of American businesses and its deepening ties to the Soviet Union, the lame-duck Eisenhower administration formally broke diplomatic relations with Cuba in January 1961.

Determined to eliminate Castro once and for all, Kennedy gave the green light that April for what became the disastrous Bay of Pigs invasion. The operation was premised on the notion that Castro maintained only very thin support among the populace and that, once the 1,400 CIA-trained commandos landed, the Cuban people would rise up and overthrow the communist autocrat. It proved a farcical plan; within two days, Castro's forces had routed and rounded up the small band of exiles, dealing Kennedy's infant presidency an embarrassing political setback. However chastened, the Democratic chief executive still could not reconcile himself to the continued existence of a Soviet beachhead in the Western

MRBM LAUNCH SITE 1
SAN CRISTOBAL, CUBA
23 OCTOBER 1962

7. **Photographic evidence of a medium-range ballistic missile site at San Cristobal, Cuba, October 1962.**

hemisphere. He subsequently ordered a renewed covert campaign to sabotage and subvert the Castro government, while the CIA, with White House approval, launched a series of ever more bizarre plans to assassinate Cuba's 'Maximum Leader'. It is difficult to dispute Castro's retrospective observation that: 'If the United States had not been bent on liquidating the Cuban revolution, there would not have been an October crisis.'

The October crisis, or the Cuban Missile Crisis as it is more commonly known, constitutes the most dangerous Soviet–American confrontation of the entire Cold War, the one in which the two superpowers – and the world – came closest to the devastation of nuclear war. The crisis broke on 14 October 1962, when a U-2 reconnaissance plane photographed some intermediate-range missile sites under construction in Cuba. Two days later, the intelligence community presented the president with incontrovertible photographic evidence that the Soviet Union had placed missiles in Cuba. Those images offered an alarming picture: Cuba had already received between 16 and 32 missiles from the Soviet Union, both Intermediate Range Ballistic Missiles (IRBMs), with a striking range of 2,200 miles, and Medium Range Ballistic Missiles (MRBMs), with a striking range of 1,020 miles. The CIA estimated that the missiles would probably be operational within a week and, once mounted with nuclear warheads, be capable of inflicting as many as 80 million casualties if launched against major US cities. Judging this startling development an exceedingly grave threat to US security, Kennedy constituted an Executive Committee, or ExCom, of his National Security Council to provide him with advice and build a consensus behind the agonizing decisions he knew he would soon have to make. The president and his inner circle were agreed, from the first, about the absolute unacceptability of nuclear missiles in Cuba and hence upon the need for their prompt removal. The most daunting question, and the one upon which the virtually round-the-clock meetings of the ExCom pivoted, concerned what means could most reliably be employed to achieve that end – without triggering a nuclear conflict.

Why had Khrushchev rolled the dice in so blatantly provocative a manner? Available evidence now suggests that, in May 1962, the Soviet premier decided upon the risky gambit of deploying nuclear missiles to Cuba for several reinforcing reasons. He sought, first of all, to deter a US invasion of Cuba, thereby affording protection to a regime that had cast its lot with the Soviet Union. By so doing, he could also deflect the challenge posed by an increasingly hostile China and reclaim the Kremlin's historic position as the military and ideological fountainhead of the world's socialist revolutionary forces. Additionally, and perhaps most importantly, Khrushchev saw in the beleaguered Cuban revolution a fortuitous opportunity to close the wide missile gap between the Soviet Union and the United States. 'The Americans had surrounded our country with military bases and threatened us with nuclear weapons, and now they would learn just what it feels like to have enemy missiles pointing at you,' he later mused, 'we'd be doing nothing but giving them a little of their own medicine.'

In view of the huge disparity in mid-1962 between the deliverable nuclear warheads possessed by the Americans and those possessed by the Soviets – an imbalance in the order of 17 to 1 – Khrushchev's Cuba missiles, although they would not have altered the overall strategic balance, would have doubled, or possibly tripled, the number of Soviet warheads capable of hitting US targets. Psychologically and politically, if not strategically, those missiles would have altered the dynamics of the superpower relationship to the disadvantage of the United States.

After Cuba agreed to the Kremlin offer in June, the Soviets began clandestinely to insert a substantial military force on to the island. In addition to the planned IRBM and MRBM installations, Moscow provided surface-to-air missiles for protection of those sites, 42 light IL-28 bombers, another 42 MIG-21 fighter-interceptors, and 42,000 Soviet troops. Unknown to any American analysts at the time, Soviet forces in Cuba were also armed with tactical, or short-range, nuclear weapons that local commanders had the authorization to use in case of a US invasion. When McNamara learned, decades later, that nine tactical nuclear weapons had been present in Cuba in October 1962, he exclaimed: 'This is horrifying. It meant that had a U.S. invasion been carried out . . . there was a 99 percent probability that nuclear war would have been initiated.'

Invasion was, in fact, one of the main options weighed by Kennedy's ExCom in the early days of the crisis. Although a full-scale US invasion of Cuba had strong proponents, including the Joint Chiefs of Staff, as did the notion of a surgical airstrike designed to obliterate the missiles, JFK chose a more prudent, and considerably less risky, course. He decided to implement a naval blockade, or quarantine, of Cuba to prevent any additional military shipments reaching the island. On 22 October, the president went on national television to explain the gravity of the threat, and outline his quarantine decision, to the American people. If any Soviet missiles were launched from Cuban soil against any targets anywhere in the Western hemisphere, Kennedy emphasized, the United States would regard it 'as an attack by the Soviet Union on the United States, requiring a full retaliatory response upon the Soviet Union'. On 24 October, US policy-makers breathed a collective sigh of relief when Soviet ships halted short of the quarantine line, averting a feared confrontation. Secretary of State Rusk famously quipped: 'Remember when you report this – that eyeball to eyeball, they blinked first.'

Yet the crisis was hardly over. Construction work on the missile sites continued; a potential invasion force of 140,000 troops assembled in south Florida; and Kennedy placed US strategic nuclear forces on high alert. In a letter to Kennedy of 26 October, Khrushchev struck a conciliatory tone. Although condemning the US blockade as an act of naval piracy, the Soviet leader evinced a willingness to remove the missiles from Cuba in return for a US pledge not to invade the island. In a confusing twist, he made public the next day another, more belligerent letter to JFK in which the Russian ruler suddenly raised the price for a settlement, calling not just for a no-invasion pledge but also for the removal of US Jupiter missiles from Turkey. Those missiles, which had become operational earlier in the year, served as a particularly galling symbol to the Soviets of their nuclear inferiority – even though they were considered by US nuclear specialists to be of minuscule strategic value.

On 28 October, at the very moment when the situation appeared to be spinning out of control, American and Soviet negotiators reached a tentative resolution. With the president's brother, Attorney General Robert F. Kennedy, playing a key role, the United States offered a compromise settlement, based largely upon Khrushchev's first letter, that proved acceptable to Moscow. The Soviets thus agreed to remove the missiles from Cuba; for their part, the Americans pledged not to invade the island. Khrushchev immediately revealed the outlines of the agreement in a radio broadcast. In an important addendum, which was not made public at the time, Khrushchev indicated via a personal letter to Kennedy his understanding that the future removal of the Jupiter missiles from Turkey also constituted a basic element of the deal, as Robert Kennedy had earlier promised a Soviet representative. At US insistence, however, the Jupiter removal was not to be tied explicitly to the Cuban imbroglio because the Turkish missiles were technically under NATO, and not American, control.

Over the past four decades, scholars, policy analysts, and former governmental officials have vigorously debated every aspect of this near-catastrophe, often varying sharply in their interpretive judgements. While some have touted Kennedy's masterful crisis management and remarkable cool under fire, others have blasted the American president for his willingness to court nuclear war, and the almost certain deaths of tens of millions of Americans, Soviets, Cubans, and Europeans, over the emplacement of missiles that did not fundamentally alter the prevailing nuclear balance. Former Secretary of State Dean Acheson, who sat in on the ExCom meetings, later attributed JFK's Cuban success to 'plain dumb luck'. That may be the most apt coda for this whole affair, especially when one recognizes how close the world actually came to nuclear war in October 1962. By the same token, one must acknowledge that Kennedy's instinctive caution and prudence, in the face of fierce pressure from his military advisers for a more aggressive response, was instrumental to the peaceful denouement of an affair fraught with unparalleled danger.

The Cuban Missile Crisis certainly demonstrates – as did the earlier crises over the Taiwan Strait and Berlin – the centrality of the nuclear imbalance at this stage of the Cold War. US decision-makers felt supremely confident that they could force the Soviets to back down in any confrontation; their nation's overwhelming

8. Khrushchev and Castro embrace at the United Nations, September 1960.

nuclear superiority served, in this sense, as the ultimate trump card, a fact of atomic age life understood every bit as much in Moscow as in Washington. Yet both sides also realized that the huge American edge in deliverable nuclear warheads was a temporary phenomenon. US experts fully expected the Soviets to achieve relative nuclear parity in the near future; Soviet defence planners, for their part, were determined to close the gap as expeditiously as possible. Reflecting the mix of bitterness and steely resolve pervasive among the Kremlin elite, Deputy Foreign Minister Vassily Kuznetsov warned a US diplomat shortly after the missile crisis: 'You Americans will never be able to do this to us again.'

That vow proved a prophetic guide to subsequent Soviet policy. Moscow embarked on a concerted effort to build up its nuclear stockpile, augment its bomber fleet, and improve its missile programme in the aftermath of the showdown in the Caribbean. Within a few years, the Soviets had developed a sophisticated new generation of ICBMs that gave them what they had not possessed when Kennedy forced Khrushchev's hasty retreat from Cuba: the near certain ability to inflict horrific damage on the American homeland in any nuclear exchange. That accomplishment, confirmed by the mid-1960s, heralded a permanent alteration in the nuclear arms equation, and a consequent change in the nature of the Cold War. Once both sides had the ability to inflict unacceptable damage on the other, or so the thinking of nuclear strategists went, then neither side could afford to risk a nuclear exchange. According to this hopeful logic, soon tagged the doctrine of Mutually Assured Destruction (or MAD), the possession by each superpower of huge nuclear stockpiles actually enhanced global security by rendering nuclear conflict irrationally self-destructive for each.

The Cuban Missile Crisis deserves recognition as one of the Cold War's critical turning points for other reasons as well. Having peered into the nuclear abyss, US and Soviet leaders recognized the need to avoid future Cuba-type confrontations and began to take some significant steps in that direction. In June 1963, a 'hot line' was installed in the Kremlin and the White House to facilitate direct communication in times of crisis. In August 1963, the United States and the Soviet Union signed a limited test ban treaty, eliminating all but underground nuclear tests. Two months later, they also endorsed a UN resolution prohibiting nuclear weapons from space. Even the rhetoric on both sides cooled notably, with Khrushchev applauding Kennedy's conciliatory speech at American University in June 1963, in which the president said that more attention should be directed 'to our common interests and to the means by which differences can be resolved'.

The Cuban Missile Crisis also had an impact on the Western alliance. Some of America's NATO partners, particularly France and West Germany, drew the unsettling lesson that Washington would always act in its own interests in any confrontation with the Soviet Union, even if it was European lives that lay on the front lines. Although standing four-square with the United States throughout the crisis, and exulting in the easing of East–West tensions that followed, they were unnerved by the Kennedy administration's decision to inform, rather than consult, them about US actions. French President Charles de Gaulle feared that France might someday face 'annihilation without representation'. Convinced that his nation's security, and that of Europe as a whole, would be better served by a more independent French foreign policy, he moved to develop an independent French nuclear force, distanced France from the American-dominated NATO military structure, and cemented the connection between Paris and Bonn. All those trends carried profound implications for the triangular relationship between the Soviet Union, the United States, and America's loyal but restive European allies. So, too, would the longest, bloodiest, and most controversial conflict of the entire Cold War era.

9. French general and political leader Charles de Gaulle.

Charles de Gaulle

The French general who headed the Free French government-in-exile during World War II, de Gaulle served as president of France immediately following liberation, returning to power again in 1958. As president of France from 1958 until his retirement in 1969, the prideful, arrogant, and intensely nationalistic de Gaulle strove to develop a leadership role for France within Europe that would be independent of the Anglo-American axis. The January 1963 Franco-German treaty of cooperation, mutual support, and strategic coordination, which he initiated, served as the centrepiece of de Gaulle's plans for an invigorated continental bloc. In 1966, he withdrew France from NATO's integrated command structure – but not from the alliance itself.

Vietnam: the Cold War's tragic sideshow

The Vietnam War presents the student of the Cold War with a great paradox. On the one hand, the United States and the Soviet Union seemed to be moving towards a more stable and much safer relationship in the aftermath of the Cuban Missile Crisis. The Cold War glacier truly seemed to be melting. Yet, at the same moment that the process of incipient detente was unfolding, the United States was inching closer to war on the distant Southeast Asian periphery – for self-professed Cold War reasons. By the time of Kennedy's assassination in November 1963, the United States had sent 16,000 military advisers to South Vietnam, permitted those advisers to participate in combat operations against Viet Cong insurgents, initiated covert operations against North Vietnam, and significantly deepened its commitment to preserve a non-communist regime in South Vietnam. By the time Lyndon B. Johnson left office five years later, over half a million US troops were stationed in South Vietnam, bogged down in a ferocious war of attrition against a determined and elusive foe that was receiving diplomatic backing and material support from both Moscow and Beijing. The Johnson White House faced by then not only an American polity that was profoundly divided about the efficacy, and morality, of the Vietnam War but a 'Free World' alliance system that was similarly divided. By the late 1960s, in some cases much earlier, such key allies as Canada, France, Great Britain, Germany, the Netherlands, Italy, and Japan openly questioned the relevance of America's costly exertions in Indo-China to common Cold War interests and policies.

The underlying reasons behind Washington's fateful decision to intervene in Vietnam with massive military force, however misguided they might appear in retrospect, are not difficult to discern. They lie almost entirely within the realm of Cold War fears. In the broadest sense, US intervention derived from a determination to contain China and to prove simultaneously, for the sake both of allies and adversaries, the credibility of American power and the sanctity of American commitments. It is difficult to disagree with historian George C. Herring's overall assessment that 'U.S. involvement in Vietnam was a logical, if not inevitable, outgrowth of a world view and a policy – the policy of containment – that Americans in and out of government accepted without serious question for more than two decades.' That policy, it bears emphasizing, sought the containment not just of the Soviet Union but also of China – and of any Third World revolutionary movements, especially those of a strongly anti-Western bent, that would likely align with one or both of those leading communist states.

By the early 1960s, China had in many respects supplanted the Soviet Union as America's most feared adversary. Of the two communist giants, it appeared far the more militant, hostile, and belligerent. The post-Cuban Missile Crisis period, which produced a thaw in US–Soviet relations, brought no respite to US–Chinese tensions. Indeed, China's initiation of a brief border war with India in October 1962 just reaffirmed US suspicions about Beijing's aggressive proclivities. National security planners of the Kennedy and Johnson administrations were convinced that the increasingly virulent Sino-Soviet split had just emboldened Beijing's leaders, making them more, rather than less, aggressive, adventuristic, and unpredictable. American leaders made explicit, on numerous occasions, the connection between China's presumed expansionist tendencies and the need for US intervention in Vietnam. 'Over this war – and all Asia – is another reality,' Johnson declared in an important April 1965 speech: 'the deepening shadow of communist China. The contest in Vietnam is part of a wider pattern of [Chinese] aggressive purposes'. Defense Secretary McNamara, in a background session with the press that same month, remarked that the alternative to fighting in Vietnam was a Chinese-dominated Southeast Asia, which would mean a 'Red Asia'. If the United States withdrew from Vietnam, he warned, a complete shift would occur in the world balance of power.

The determination of the United States to demonstrate its credibility as a power that met aggression with steely resolve and honoured its commitments to allies merged seamlessly with the anti-China strand in US policy. In a typical assessment, National Security Adviser McGeorge Bundy warned Johnson in early 1965: 'The international prestige of the United States, and a substantial part of our influence, are directly at risk in Vietnam.' Johnson and his top advisers, like a whole generation of American Cold Warriors, were convinced that US credibility must be preserved at almost any cost. It was the indispensable glue holding together America's entire Cold War alliance system as well as the principal deterrent to communist aggression.

The imperatives of domestic politics also influenced US policy decisions. Early in his presidency, Kennedy confessed to a journalist about the deteriorating situation in Vietnam: 'I can't give up a piece of territory like that to the communists, and get the American people to reelect me.' Both JFK and LBJ worried that the loss of South Vietnam to communism would ignite a political firestorm at home that would paralyse the country – and destroy their respective presidencies. According to political adviser Jack Valenti, Johnson was convinced that Republicans and conservative Democrats together would have 'torn him in pieces' had he failed to hold the line against communism in Southeast Asia. He worried as well that his ambitious domestic reform programme could be derailed in Congress should a humiliating defeat in Vietnam transpire under his watch.

If the forces propelling the United States towards war in Indo-China were strong, they were by no means irresistible. The Johnson administration, which crossed the Rubicon in early 1965 with its twin decisions to inaugurate a full-scale bombing campaign against North Vietnam and to dispatch US combat troops to South Vietnam, could have opted instead for a negotiated settlement, as the Kennedy administration did in Laos in 1961–2. Powerful constituencies at home, especially within the Congress and the establishment media, as well as leading voices in allied capitals, urged exactly such a course on first Kennedy and then Johnson. In August 1963, French President de Gaulle publicly called for a neutralized Vietnam, offering the United States a face-saving salve. Neither Kennedy nor Johnson, however, would accept a diplomatic alternative that they equated with defeat. American leaders portrayed their stubborn resolve in South Vietnam as fully consistent with previous Cold War commitments. 'The challenge we face in Southeast Asia today', Johnson insisted in an August 1964 speech, 'is the same challenge that we have faced with courage and that we have met with strength in Greece and Turkey, in Berlin and Korea, and in Lebanon and China.' The defence of Saigon, Secretary of State Dean Rusk frequently stressed, was just as important to the security of the 'Free World' as the defence of West Berlin.

From the first, key NATO allies dissented. Most did not consider the prospective victory of communist forces in Vietnam in the same apocalyptic terms as their American partners. In contrast to policy-makers in Washington, they viewed Southeast Asia as peripheral to Western security, downplayed the existence of the Chinese regional threat that so exercised the Americans, and disputed the relevance of a South Vietnamese regime mired in corruption and incompetence to the overall position of the West in the ongoing Cold War. America's allies mocked, though rarely in public, the US effort to make the defence of Saigon synonymous with the defence of Berlin.

One did not, in short, have to stand outside the Cold War consensus that still prevailed both within American society and within the states and societies that made up the wider Western alliance to oppose Johnson's lurch towards open-ended conflict in Indo-China. Not only the imperious and fiercely independent de Gaulle counselled against intervention, but Britain's Harold Wilson, Canada's Lester Pearson, and other loyal allied leaders. The United States chose, however, to turn a deaf ear to those voices of caution and restraint. Haunted by fears about the consequences – strategic, psychological, and political – of defeat in Vietnam, Johnson and his top advisers quite consciously chose war over diplomatic accommodation.

Between 1965 and 1968, the Johnson administration poured resources and men into South Vietnam in a fruitless effort to crush a popular insurgency while trying simultaneously to prop up a succession of unpopular and ineffectual governments in Saigon. Moscow and Beijing, for their part, provided Hanoi with critically needed military aid and materiel, thereby further complicating the American task while lending an additional East–West cast to the conflict. As the war dragged on inconclusively, the ranks of the dissidents swelled – within the United States and abroad – and the Cold War consensus that had sustained US overseas commitments for the previous two decades began to fracture. The enemy's massive

Tet offensive of early 1968 baldly exposed the contradictions of US military strategy in Vietnam – and, even more fundamentally, the limits of American power.

The decade bracketed by the Taiwan and Berlin crises of 1958 and the Tet offensive of 1968 marked a major transformation in the Cold War. The East–West struggle arguably reached its most hazardous turn between 1958 and 1962, culminating with the epochal Cuban Missile Crisis. Thereafter, Soviet–American relations experienced a thaw, only to be rocked again by US escalation in Vietnam. Yet, despite the Vietnam War, the United States and the Soviet Union managed to avert another major confrontation throughout the mid- and late 1960s while maintaining at least some of the positive momentum engendered by the post-Cuban Missile Crisis rapprochement. By 1968, the superpowers were actually inching towards a historic agreement on the limitation of strategic arms. The changing nature of the Cold War's domestic dynamics – in both West and East – helped to make such a breakthrough possible.

Chapter 6
Cold wars at home

The Cold War exerted so profound and so multi-faceted an impact on the structure of international politics and state-to-state relations that it has become customary to label the 1945–90 period 'the Cold War era'. That designation becomes even more fitting when one considers the powerful mark that the Soviet–American struggle for world dominance and ideological supremacy left *within* many of the world's nation-states, the subject of this chapter. Every major development that transpired between 1945 and 1990 cannot, of course, be tied to the Cold War. By the same token, so much *was* influenced and shaped by the Cold War that one simply cannot write a history of the second half of the 20th century without a systematic appreciation of the powerful, oft-times distorting repercussions of the superpower conflict on the world's states and societies.

Its domestic repercussions have received much less systematic attention from scholars than the Cold War's international dynamics. This chapter offers simply a very general, broad-brush survey of this enormous topic. It suggests some of the ways in which the Cold War affected the internal constellation of forces in the Third World, Europe, and the United States.

The Third World: decolonization, state formation, and Cold War geopolitics

The emergence of dozens of newly independent nation-states across the breadth of the Third World, together with the occasionally bloody, invariably conflict-ridden, process of decolonization that brought them forth, not only coincided temporally with the Cold War but was inextricably shaped by that same Cold War. Indeed, it was the all-encompassing struggle for global power and influence between the United States, the Soviet Union, and their respective allies that gave birth to the very term 'Third World'. A convenient political catchphrase that rather loosely lumped together the predominantly poor, non-white, and uncommitted areas of the planet, Third World originally connoted an arena of contestation between West and East, the so-called First and Second Worlds. Cold War pressures sometimes exacerbated, on other occasions facilitated, the transition from colonialism to independence. Although the particular impact of the Cold War varied greatly from one end-of-empire struggle to another, the superpower contest loomed always as a key external variable. Any history of decolonization would be incomplete if it failed to examine the manifold ways in which the superpower conflict impinged upon the process – from the South and Southeast Asian freedom movements of the mid- and late 1940s, which opened the decolonization era, through the resistance of Africans to Portuguese colonial rule in the early and mid-1970s, which brought it to a close.

The formation of new, post-colonial states throughout much of Asia, Africa, and the Middle East, and parts of the Caribbean as well, also unfolded against the ever-present backdrop of the Cold War. The shape, cohesion, and vitality of those states; the internal configurations of power within them; their ability to command international attention and prestige; their leaders' prospects for securing external resources, capital, and technical assistance to meet economic development priorities or for garnering military assistance to bolster defence needs – all were affected significantly by the Cold War. In so many respects, the history of post-World War II state formation in the Third World – like the history of decolonization – simply cannot be written without paying careful, systematic attention to that key external variable.

The Cold War presented aspiring Third World leaders with a complex range of problems, challenges, and opportunities. This initially became evident during the anti-colonial struggles in early postwar Southeast Asia. Ho Chi Minh and Sukarno each appealed to the United States for assistance immediately following Japan's surrender, framing their requests in terms of America's historic support for self-determination. Yet each was quickly disheartened to learn that the Truman administration's commitment to its Cold War allies in Europe took precedence, foreclosing, at least initially, any diplomatic or material commitment to their respective independence movements. Ho, a veteran Comintern agent and founding member of the Indochina Communist Party, turned to the Soviet Union and the People's Republic of China for backing, which he began to receive early in 1950. Sukarno, on the other hand, proved his anti-communist *bona fides* by suppressing an internal communist bid to gain control of the larger Indonesian independence movement. By suppressing the Madiun rebellion of 1948, Indonesian nationalists demonstrated the moderate character of their movement; that forceful action formed part of a quite conscious strategy aimed at courting Western, and especially American, backing. The strategy ultimately succeeded insofar as the Truman administration pressed the Netherlands the next year to grant independence to what it judged to be a relatively reliable and firmly anti-communist Indonesian leadership.

The radically divergent trajectories of the comparable bids for national self-governance mounted by Vietnamese and Indonesian nationalists illustrate clearly the importance of Cold War dynamics *inside* Third World societies. These cases also illuminate the different choices available to indigenous statesmen as they tried to navigate the treacherous shoals of great power politics. At the extremes, these leaders could court American backing by demonstrating or pledging their anti-communist convictions, moderate character, and pro-Western leanings; or, alternatively, they could bid for Soviet or Chinese support by highlighting their revolutionary, anti-Western credentials.

In the essentially bipolar world that all Third World independence movements from the mid-1940s through to the mid-1970s faced, the pressure to line up with one or the other ideological camp cum military alliance system was hard to deflect – especially since concrete benefits could flow, or be blocked, as a result of the choice made. The more contested the bid for independence, the greater the need of the independence-seekers for support from one or the other of the two blocs. When anti-colonial coalitions fractured, moreover, such as in the Congo in 1960 and Angola in 1974–5, the temptation for competing factions to draw support from different superpower patrons proved irresistible. The particular visions that nationalist leaders had for the future, which often encompassed far-reaching socioeconomic transformations within their native lands, further complicated the choices forced on them by the pressures of the superpower conflict. Decamping in the Western power bloc, with its deep-seated suspicions of those inclined to march to a socialist drumbeat, could constrict certain domestic political and development paths, compromising the freedom of choice that founding national elites invariably crave. Decamping in the socialist bloc, on the other hand, would surely minimize, if not preclude entirely, the option of coaxing dollars and support from the world's richest and most powerful nation.

With independence, newly established Third World states faced an equally acute set of dilemmas. Some actively sought alignment with the United States because a formal commitment to the West seemed to comport best with key domestic needs. In the case of Pakistan, for example, its governing elites pursued an American connection with vigour from their fragile country's earliest days, becoming a formal ally in the mid-1950s through the negotiation of a bilateral security agreement with Washington and membership in two multilateral pacts. The US connection afforded Pakistan protection less from the Soviet Union than from India, its principal regional rival, or so top Pakistani decision-makers believed. It thus offered a means to help ensure the survival of a most precarious experiment in nation-building, given Pakistan's ethnically, linguistically, and geographically divided polity, while strengthening the dominant position within that state of the Punjabi ethnic group that had pushed most aggressively for US aid and Western alignment. Throughout the decade and a half that followed, Pakistan's Cold War commitments, and the military and economic aid that resulted from them, powerfully shaped the internal constellation of forces within the country. The alliance with the United States bolstered the Punjabi elite, and the Pakistani military in particular, at the expense of other internal contestants for power, distorting the nation's political balance nearly from its inception.

In the case of Thailand, to cite another telling example, its leaders sought an American connection for a similar mix of reasons. They coveted an external patron as part of a long-established national strategy inspired by the traditional fear of China, their huge and potentially menacing neighbour – whether communist or not. The Cold War provided Thai elites with a means to secure that external patron since their needs happened to dovetail with America's search for Third World allies. Like their counterparts in Pakistan, Thai military leaders also sought an American connection and the dollars sure to flow from it so as to tighten their own internal grip on power and to silence dissident voices. In the event, the course of modern Thai history was altered in profound ways.

Although each particular circumstance naturally reveals unique features, a broader pattern plainly obtains in which those Third World nations that opted for Western alignment did so more for domestic reasons than out of a fear of communism, and in which subsequent internal developments within those states were deeply influenced as a consequence. Such varied countries as Iraq, Iran, Saudi Arabia, Turkey, Pakistan, the Philippines, Ceylon, South Korea, and Thailand – to mention just some of the more prominent – each found their domestic priorities, available resources, and internal balance of forces severely affected by the decisions of their leaders to align formally or informally with the West. Some were newly emergent states, of course, the product of independence struggles; others were much older states whose status as self-governing entities had been compromised but never completely extinguished by the Western imperium. Yet, despite those widely divergent histories, the strong imprint left by the Cold War on each remains unmistakable.

The strategy of studied non-alignment appealed to another group of Third World leaders, those who believed that important national goals could be more effectively advanced by eschewing a formal commitment to either West or East. Indonesia's Sukarno, Egypt's Gamal Abdel Nasser, Ghana's Kwame Nkrumah, and India's Jawaharlal Nehru, among others, consciously strove for a position of independence for their nations from either of the Cold War power blocs. The complex factors that lay behind the latter's calculations in pursuing a non-aligned course are broadly illustrative. 'Once foreign relations go out of our hand into the charge of somebody else,' warned Nehru, 'to that extent and in that measure you are not independent.' India's first prime minister was convinced that his young nation could maximize its international stature and influence in world councils by assuming the role of a third force in international affairs. By so doing, moreover, Nehru's ruling Congress Party could avoid the inevitable alienation of some powerful political forces within India's remarkably diverse polity that would have resulted from a formal commitment to either West or East. By remaining unattached to the American or the Soviet spheres of influence, additionally, Indian planners calculated that they might be able to attract needed developmental assistance from both camps. 'Even in accepting economic help,' a realistic Nehru confided to an aide, 'it is not a wise policy to put all our eggs in one basket.' Sukarno, Nasser, Nkrumah, and others would have heartily agreed with that sentiment. Much to the consternation of American Cold Warriors, who frequently exhibited a you-are-with-us-or-you-are-against-us mentality, Washington was indeed compelled to compete for the non-aligned, or neutral, nations of the Third World.

One must, in sum, acknowledge the agency of Third World actors as they tried to harness the dominant international reality of their age, the Cold War, to maximize potential benefits – or at least to minimize potential damages. One must also recognize, however, that many of the Cold War's consequences for Third World peoples and societies proved as unanticipated as they were beyond the control of any local actors. In that regard, it is worth re-emphasizing here that the Third World emerged as early as 1950 as the Cold War's principal battlefield. Conflicts with local roots – from Korea, the Congo, and Vietnam to Angola, Afghanistan, and Nicaragua – became exponentially more costly because the superpower conflict became superimposed upon them. It is worth recalling here that the vast bulk of the estimated 20 million who died in the wars that raged across the globe between 1945 and 1990 were victims of Third World conflicts, most of which were at least indirectly connected to the Cold War.

The Cold War's impact within Europe

The Cold War's impact within Europe offers the starkest of contrasts. If the Soviet–American contest can be blamed for a good deal of the warfare, devastation, and instability that wracked the newly emerging areas between 1945 and 1990, then it conversely deserves much of the credit for the unprecedented era of peace, prosperity, and stability experienced by Europeans. Ironically, an ideological and geopolitical struggle that began as a conflict over the fate of Europe actually wound up not just sparing Europe but laying the essential foundation for the most sustained economic boom in European history. That boom was accompanied and made possible by a durable peace across the continent and rapid movement towards political and economic integration within Western Europe, each development abetted by the Cold War. The 'Golden Age' of capitalist expansion and productivity that spanned from the late 1940s through to the early 1970s essentially coincided with the first two and a half decades of the Cold War – and was fostered, in significant measure, by that same Cold War. Those years witnessed 'the most dramatic, rapid and profound revolution in human affairs of which history has record', in the apt assessment of historian Eric Hobsbawm. 'For many of those who had lived through the Depression and war,' adds historian John Young, 'Western Europe seemed a promised land.'

Economic, political, and security trends proved mutually reinforcing in Cold War Europe. The approximately $13 billion pumped into Western Europe by American Marshall Plan aid between 1948 and 1952 certainly helped spur the great postwar boom, even if economic historians continue to debate the precise weight that should be assigned to the American contribution. The US security umbrella and US support for and encouragement of both West Germany's integration into Western Europe and parallel movement towards broader regional integration also played an instrumental role. Western European statesmen sometimes followed the American lead but just as frequently took the lead themselves, seizing the opportunities afforded by the Cold War, the occupation of Germany, and the new-found US interest in European affairs to forge the kind of region-wide changes and internal economic and social reforms that they judged necessary. They and their American backers recognized from the start, as historian Herman-Josef Rupieper notes, 'that if prosperity and democracy were to flourish in the Western half of a divided Europe then the Western Europeans, with American aid and protection, would have to move toward an integrated political, military, and economic system.' Leaders of key Western European states were also keenly aware that the problem of Germany, which had plagued the security of the continent for generations, needed to be resolved so that German productivity could be harnessed for the benefit of

Europe's economic recovery without Germany again emerging as a military menace.

They acted with creativity and resolve to find solutions to those problems. In July 1952, France, Italy, the German Federal Republic, Belgium, the Netherlands, and Luxembourg formed the European Coal and Steel Community. In March 1957, in an even bolder and more significant step towards unity, the same six nations signed the Rome treaties establishing a European Economic Community (EEC) and a European Atomic Energy Community (EURATOM). A historic rapprochement between France and Germany facilitated the development of those successful supranational institutions. 'Germany and France are neighbours who waged war against each other again and again over the centuries', exclaimed West German Chancellor Konrad Adenauer, 'This was a European madness that must end once and for all.' The impressive growth rates of the EEC countries, which were in the vanguard of Western Europe's economic boom, demonstrated the tangible advantages of swapping military competition for economic cooperation. By 1960, 'the Six' accounted in tandem for a quarter of the world's industrial production and two-fifths of aggregate international trade.

Ordinary citizens of Western Europe were the prime beneficiaries of these developments. Sustained economic growth provided them with higher wages, shorter working weeks, generous social benefits, and improved health and education. The success of the productionist formula – essentially, bake a larger pie and all will benefit – also contributed to political stability, lessened traditional tension between labour and capital, and undercut the appeal of Western Europe's communist parties. Unemployment virtually disappeared, averaging just 2.9% throughout Western Europe in the 1950s and a mere 1.5% in the 1960s. Compared to the past, veritable consumer paradises were created in Cold War Europe; working- and middle-class people increasingly earned sufficient incomes to attain goods that had previously been the province of the wealthy. In Italy, for example, private ownership of cars jumped from 469,000 in 1938 to 15 million in 1975. Ownership of refrigerators swelled from just 8% of British households in 1956 to 69% in 1971. By 1973, 62% of French families took annual vacations, more than double the number who did so in 1958. Tellingly, British Prime Minister Harold Macmillan appealed for votes in the general election of 1959 with the remarkable slogan: 'You've never had it so good.'

During the early postwar decades, Western European consumers significantly closed the gap that had long separated them from their American counterparts. By the 1960s, they each possessed what David Reynolds identifies as the essential attributes of consumer-oriented societies: 'mass-produced domestic goods, a growing population with soaring incomes, extended credit, and aggressive advertising'. To the extent that the Cold War was also about the battle for the hearts, minds, and stomachs of rank-and-file citizens, the spectacular success of capitalist economies during the third quarter of the 20th century substantially bolstered the political and ideological claims of the United States and its Western allies.

The concomitant shortcomings of Soviet-style command economies in Eastern Europe, which struggled to meet the basic needs of local populations, further strengthened Western claims to superiority. From the 1960s onwards, an ever-widening gap opened between material conditions in Europe's Eastern and Western halves. Following World War II, the predominantly agrarian societies east of the Elbe River underwent an abrupt transition from capitalism to socialism – under the watchful eye of Stalin. Closely emulating the Soviet model, Eastern Europe's ruling communist parties embarked on policies of rapid, forced industrialization while simultaneously subordinating nationalist impulses to the imperatives of 'proletarian internationalism', as defined by Moscow. Benefits for ordinary citizens ensued, to be sure: health care improved, diets improved, mortality rates dropped, access to education expanded,

Brezhnev Doctrine

The Soviet Politburo decided to use force to expunge the stirring of political pluralism within Czechoslovakia because of a fear about the contagion of liberalism spreading throughout Eastern Europe, thereby undermining the Kremlin's authority. On 26 September 1968, the official newspaper *Pravda* issued what came to be called the Brezhnev Doctrine to justify the invasion. It held that national leaders could pursue separate developmental paths, but only if those paths did not damage socialism within the country and did not damage the wider socialist movement. In other words, the Kremlin would set the limits on diversity within Eastern Europe.

full employment was achieved. But those gains came at a very high cost in countries in which political repression, religious persecution, suppression of individual freedoms, and tightly enforced ideological conformity became the norm, as they had long been in the Soviet Union itself. The command economies of Eastern Europe and the Soviet Union recorded impressive progress through to the end of the 1950s, actually outperforming the economies of Western Europe in terms of annual growth rates. By the 1960s, however, that growth slowed appreciably as the problems inherent in top-down planning models, along with the inability of Eastern bloc states to satisfy rising consumer demands, became increasingly evident.

Periodic efforts to liberalize the political and economic systems within individual Warsaw Pact states invariably faltered throughout the 1950s and 1960s. The Soviet Union, whether under the rigid Stalin, the more flexible Khrushchev, or the dour Brezhnev, was simply unwilling to tolerate genuine structural reform or true political diversity within its sphere of influence. The flowering, and swift demise, of the 'Prague Spring' of 1968 made the limits of liberalization painfully clear. In January of that year, Alexander Dubček, a reform-minded communist leader, assumed power in Czechoslovakia. He strove to meet the popular clamour among Czechs for greater political freedoms and meaningful economic reforms while maintaining support from the Soviet Union and unity within his ruling Communist Party. It proved an impossible balancing act. During the evening of 20 August 1968, Soviet tanks rolled into Czechoslovakia and, as in Hungary 12 years earlier, crushed a hopeful experiment with political pluralism. Wisely, the Czechs chose not to resist, doubtless sparing thousands of lives. From that point forward, there could be little doubt that Soviet control in East Europe rested ultimately on naked power, and the willingness to use it.

The year 1968 marked an important juncture in the internal history of Cold War Western Europe as well. In May, students and workers in Paris mounted a series of demonstrations that nearly toppled the de Gaulle government. The French protests were only the most dramatic of a series of challenges to prevailing power structures that swept Western Europe, as well as the United States, in 1968. Although each had its local particularities, the flowering of a youth culture, a 'New Left', and an iconoclastic, anti-authoritarian spirit within most of the Western democracies suggests common bonds among them. The very success of the Cold War order in Western Europe had, it seemed, spawned a new generation that took the principal fruits of that order – peace, stability, material bounty, enhanced social benefits and educational opportunities – for granted. In France, in Italy, in West Germany, and elsewhere, this new generation, galvanized partly by the unpopular American intervention in Vietnam, began to question some of the core verities of the Cold War. Did the containment of communism necessitate bloody, Third World interventions? Was the Soviet Union still a threat? Was the presence of US troops and nuclear weapons on European soil still justified? Could alternative Western policies reduce the chance of a nuclear Armageddon? The Cold War military and foreign policy consensus, in the event, began to erode within now-prosperous Western Europe, along with the political order that it had fostered.

The Cold War's impact within the United States

The Cold War also left an indelible imprint on state and society within the United States. Indeed, it left hardly any aspect of American life untouched. As a direct result of the security fears induced by the communist/Soviet threat, the federal government assumed vastly enhanced power and responsibility, the 'imperial presidency' took centre stage, a substantial increase in defence spending became a permanent feature of the federal budget, and a military-industrial complex took root within American society. The broad shifts in the country's post-1945 residential patterns and occupational structures are, in significant measure, a by-product of the Cold War as well. So, too, is the co-opting of scientific and technological innovations for military-related purposes and the concomitant transformation of many top universities into leading sites of government-sponsored research. Many specific domestic priorities were similarly shaped, and in some cases explicitly justified, by the Cold War: from Eisenhower's proposed interstate highway system, to increased federal spending on education, to space exploration. Even the course of the civil rights movement was affected by the Soviet–American contest, albeit in contradictory ways. Segregationists initially tried to derail the black freedom struggle by tarring its supporters with the brush of communism. Yet those efforts were ultimately offset by the Eisenhower and Kennedy administrations' recognition that a continuation of the South's system of racial subordination and the denial of essential rights to African-Americans tarnished America's global image and thus formed an unacceptable Cold War liability.

Politically, culturally, and psychologically, too, the Cold War altered the contours of American life in manifold ways. The ideological conformity demanded by many of the nation's political elites led to a narrowing of the permissible boundaries of political discourse, placing many reform movements on the defensive and leaving some liberals vulnerable to accusations of radicalism and disloyalty. 'Red-baiting' and guilt by association became common, if deplorable, tactics in local and national elections, trade union politics, and investigations of government employees, teachers, and members of the film industry, among others. Historian Stephen J. Whitfield blames the Cold War for 'the suffocation of liberty and the debasement of culture itself' in the United States, especially during the 1950s. It fostered a repression, he argues, which 'weakened the legacy of civil liberties, impugned standards of tolerance and fair play, and tarnished the very image of a democracy'. Fellow scholars Peter J. Kuznick and James Gilbert locate the Cold War's greatest impact within the diffuse realm of social psychology: 'It persuaded millions of Americans', they write, 'to interpret their world in terms of insidious enemies at home and abroad who threatened them with nuclear and other forms of annihilation.' Widespread fear, in sum, of domestic as well as foreign enemies, stands as a key legacy of the Cold War.

Plainly, society-wide anxiety about the potential menace communism posed *within* the United States ranks as one of the most immediate and arresting manifestations of the Cold War at home. That apprehension was incubated by a particular set of elites for their own purposes. There *were* communists in the United States, to be sure, if not many of them. The American Communist Party boasted only about 32,000 members in 1950, the same year that the most notorious anti-communist, Wisconsin Senator Joseph McCarthy, first launched his sensational crusade against the presumed hordes of communists who, he charged, resided within the halls of the US Government itself. To put that figure in perspective, there were as many members of the Finnish Evangelical Lutheran Church in 1950 as there were dues-paying members of the Communist Party. There also *were* communists, or communist sympathizers, within the executive branch of the government, albeit never more than a handful. The case of Alger Hiss, a former mid-level State Department official who evidently did spy for the Soviet Union and was convicted of perjury in a closely watched 1948 trial, was the most significant.

McCarthy and other partisan politicians deliberately exaggerated the problem, however, manipulating public fears to advance their own careers. That the bombastic McCarthy singled out none other than George Marshall for particular vilification at one point is indicative of the senator's unscrupulous tactics and fundamental dishonesty. The highly respected former general and secretary of state and defence was, McCarthy declared, part of 'a conspiracy so immense and an infamy so black as to dwarf any previous such venture in the history of man'. Nor was he alone in levelling preposterous charges in order to keep political opponents on the defensive. California Congressman and Senator Richard M. Nixon, for example, Hiss's principal prosecutor, owed his rise to national prominence to the reputation he developed for pursuing communist subversives with uncommon doggedness. As Eisenhower's running mate in 1952, Nixon once excoriated Democratic presidential candidate Adlai Stevenson as an 'appeaser' who was a 'Ph.D. graduate of Dean Acheson's cowardly college of Communist containment'.

For all the deserved attention McCarthyism, and the communist witch hunt of which it formed the most extreme variant, has received from scholars, other domestic effects of the Cold War actually proved more far-reaching. The massive growth of defence spending, with its explosive effects on the overall national economy, on occupational opportunities, and on population shifts, deserves recognition as the most potent agent of change within Cold War America. During the first two decades of the Cold War, the federal government invested $776 billion in national defence, approximately 60% of the total federal budget. That percentage mounts even higher if one includes indirect defence-related expenditures. Defence needs quickly came to dominate the nation's research and development priorities, as private and university-based scientists and engineers scrambled to satisfy the government's needs – and reap lucrative contracts in the process. Wholly new or freshly invigorated industries, including communications, electronics, aircraft, computing, and space exploration, expanded along with, and in large measure because of, the Cold War. Some of these industries, in the apt words of economist Ann Markusen, 'were to irrevocably alter the American economic, occupational, and regional landscape'. Among the greatest ramifications of Cold War-driven defence spending were the burgeoning of defence plants in the south and the west at the expense of the nation's older industrial base in the northeast and midwest. California alone received more than $67 billion in defence contracts between 1951 and 1965, about 20% of the total, as the Cold War helped foster the growth of the so-called Sunbelt. It stimulated, relatedly, a major demographic shift of the American population towards the west and south and an ancillary reweighting of the scales of political power within the Congress and within the party system; both have been hallmarks of the post-World War II era.

The vast budgetary demands and multiple military obligations that the Cold War imposed upon the American populace required a mobilized and committed citizenry. US leaders from Truman onwards laboured assiduously to forge a domestic consensus supportive of the nation's new role as the world's ever-vigilant guardian against any sign of communist-inspired instability or aggression. They managed to do so with consummate skill and success through the mid-1960s, aided by what seemed unmistakable evidence of Soviet and Chinese adventurism from Eastern Europe and Berlin to Korea, Taiwan, and Cuba. As the Cold War entered its third decade, however, that consensus began to crack. The Vietnam War brought home to Americans the high – and, for a growing number, unacceptable – costs of their nation's global hegemony. The war, which spurred the largest peace movement in US history, triggered a wrenching domestic debate about the price of American globalism. That debate raged fiercely throughout the late 1960s, necessitating a reassessment at the highest levels of the American government of a global Cold War strategy that had left the country both grievously overextended and deeply divided.

Chapter 7
The rise and fall of superpower detente, 1968–79

During the 1970s, a somewhat obscure French term denoting the relaxation of tensions among former rivals suddenly entered the working vocabularies not just of statesmen but of ordinary citizens across the globe. Detente served as a convenient shorthand for the more stable and cooperative relationship being forged by the Cold War's primary protagonists, a phenomenon that came to dominate the international politics of that decade. Under the leadership, on the Soviet side, of Communist Party Chairman Leonid Brezhnev and, on the American side, of Presidents Richard M. Nixon, Gerald R. Ford, and Jimmy Carter, the two superpowers sought to regulate their continuing rivalry more effectively. They worked to lessen the danger of nuclear war through the negotiation of verifiable arms control agreements, a hallmark of detente. At the same time, the two superpowers expanded trade links, technology transfers, and scientific sharing, while also labouring to formulate a core set of 'rules' to govern their relationship.

Detente did not mean replacing the Cold War with a structure of peace, to be sure, despite the pious rhetoric from both sides that so stated. Rather, it meant managing the Cold War in a safer and more controlled manner so as to minimize the possibility either of accidental war or of a destabilizing arms spiral. Competition continued, especially in the Third World, which remained a cauldron of instability and revolutionary change. Each side, moreover, harboured a fundamentally different understanding about the meaning of detente. By the end of the 1970s, those problems had grown so severe that they brought the era of detente to an abrupt close.

The genesis of detente

Changing power realities constituted an essential prerequisite for detente. Plainly, the most important of those was the Soviet Union's achievement, by the end of the 1960s, of relative parity with the United States in strategic nuclear weapons. The product of a Herculean effort by its defence planners and scientists, the Soviet Union's massive arms build-up had, by November 1969, given it an actual numerical advantage over the United States in ICBMs – 1,140 to 1,054. Although the Americans still held a sizable edge in terms of overall nuclear arsenal, thanks to continuing superiority in submarine-launched missiles and nuclear-capable long-range bombers, the trend towards a rough equivalence was by then unmistakable. Two decades of overwhelming US nuclear superiority had come to an end, a fact that held profound implications for future relations between the superpowers. The relative decline not only of America's military power but of its economic health and vitality as well, trends exacerbated by resource-draining conflict in Vietnam and the economic resurgence of Western Europe and Japan, formed another important precondition for detente. Simply put, the United States no longer had the economic wherewithal, or political will, to sustain the policy of preponderance that had characterized its approach to the Cold War ever since the late 1940s. Finally, the onset of rising tensions between the Soviet Union and China, punctuated by border clashes between their troops and the serious possibility of actual war between the two communist rivals, provided another incentive to place the Soviet–American relationship on a sounder footing.

A national security strategy aimed at lessening tensions with the Soviet Union appealed to US policy planners on several grounds.

Above all, it seemed the most reasonable way to reduce the dangers of nuclear conflict with a now much more formidably armed rival. Detente, moreover, especially if it led to concrete arms control agreements, could lessen the pressure on a US defence budget already overburdened by the costly war in Vietnam. Bowing to that logic, Johnson signalled his administration's intention to enter into arms control negotiations with the Soviet Union in 1967. In June of that year, he met with Soviet Premier Alexsei Kosygin at a mini-summit in Glassboro, New Jersey, to discuss nuclear issues and other pressing bilateral problems. Johnson had tentatively planned to visit Moscow for further talks with Soviet leaders during the second half of 1968, only to have the trip scuttled in the aftermath of the Soviet military crackdown in Czechoslovakia.

With his assumption of the presidency in January 1969, Richard Nixon embraced detente with renewed vigour. It constituted a core element of the recalibrated Cold War strategy he was determined to implement. Along with his chief foreign policy aide, National Security Adviser Henry A. Kissinger, Nixon worried that the United States had become dangerously overextended globally, its resources stretched perilously thin. The Vietnam War served, in their view, as but the most alarming symptom of a much larger problem. 'We were becoming like other nations in the need to recognize that our power, while vast, had limits', Kissinger recalled in his memoirs. 'Our resources were no longer infinite in relation to our problems; instead, we had to set priorities, both intellectual and material.' The overriding priority for Nixon and Kissinger remained the containment of the one nation that possessed sufficient power to endanger US national security. Although he had risen to political fame in large part due to his reputation as a crusading anti-communist, the pragmatic Nixon no longer saw communism's ideological appeal as a serious threat. It was Soviet power, pure and simple, that now concerned him. 'The problem of our age', as the like-minded Kissinger phrased it, 'is to manage the emergence of the Soviet Union as a superpower.' Geopolitics trumped ideology; it was, for Nixon and Kissinger, the true currency of international affairs.

A policy of detente with the Soviet Union flowed naturally from their shared geopolitical vision, as did the hoped-for rapprochement with China. The Nixon administration aimed to restrain Moscow's nuclear arms build-up and reduce both the costs of competition and the risks of war through arms control negotiations. By simultaneously securing Moscow's *de facto* acceptance of the existing world order, the administration could help check the Soviet penchant for an adventuristic foreign policy in the Third World. If it could, at the same time, engineer an opening to long-isolated China, the United States could then play the two communist rivals off against each other, thrusting itself into the position of strategic pivot in the triangular relationship among the three powers. It was a bold plan, formulated at a time when the Vietnam War's crippling costs at home and abroad necessitated some readjustment in US Cold War strategy. Nixon hoped that implementation of the plan might also facilitate a graceful American exit from Vietnam, still the nation's most immediate foreign policy problem. A significant political pay-off beckoned as well. If Nixon could forge less conflict-ridden relationships with the Soviet Union and China, while extricating the United States from Vietnam, his re-election in 1972 would be virtually guaranteed, his reputation as a statesman assured.

The Soviet Union desired an improvement in bilateral relations for its own reasons. Fearful of the growing military threat posed by China, the Russians calculated that a relaxation of tensions with the United States would enable them to concentrate on that much more immediate menace to their security. In addition, arms control agreements with the United States would confirm the Soviet Union's status as a co-equal superpower while locking in its hard-won achievement of nuclear parity before any new technological breakthroughs allowed the United States to recapture its previous lead. It is difficult to overestimate the importance that the Kremlin leadership accorded to matters of status and respect in this regard. As Foreign Minister Gromyko proclaimed proudly to the 24th Communist Party Congress in 1971: 'Today there is no question of any importance which can be decided without the Soviet Union or in opposition to it. . . . The political significance of a stable strategic balance is indisputable . . . it is the guarantee not only of the security of the two sides, but international security as a whole.' More specific needs might also be met by pursuing a relationship of peaceful co-existence with the United States, including expanded access to US grain and technology and facilitation of a settlement of nagging European problems, such as Berlin. Brezhnev, Kosygin, Gromyko, and their Politburo associates remained confident, at this juncture, that history lay on the side of the socialist world; they accepted detente not out of weakness, but as a sign of their growing power. As Brezhnev succinctly, and astutely, put it in a 1975 speech: 'Detente became possible because a new correlation of forces in the world arena has been established.'

The flowering of detente

On 19 October 1969, Nixon set a date for talks with the Soviet Union on a strategic arms limitation treaty (SALT). The opening round began that November, alternating between Helsinki and Vienna. Almost immediately, though, the negotiations bogged down in mutual suspicion and technical arcana. Nixon's effort to link progress in the SALT talks to Soviet cooperation in pressuring North Vietnam to reach a diplomatic accommodation with the United States posed one strain, at least until Nixon gave up the attempted linkage. A more nettlesome problem arose over the different categories of nuclear weapons – specifically, over whether the proposed agreement should be confined to long-range missiles, or whether medium-range US missiles deployed in Europe, and just as capable of hitting Soviet territory, should be included as well. Fresh technological innovations presented negotiators with another complex challenge. The advent of MIRVs (multiple independently targetable re-entry vehicles), which allowed numerous nuclear warheads to be mounted on a single missile, promised to deepen significantly the destructive capabilities of each side's nuclear arsenals. The development of anti-ballistic missiles (ABMs) raised the theoretical possibility of defensive systems that could repulse nuclear missile attacks and thus negate the other side's striking power. In May 1971, Soviet and American negotiators finally achieved a breakthrough. Essentially, the Americans agreed to grant the Soviets a 3-to-2 edge in ICBMs, the Soviets chose to ignore the nuclear missiles that could be launched from Western Europe, and both parties decided not to ban MIRVs. That compromise paved the way for a gala summit meeting and treaty-signing ceremony in Moscow the next year.

Peace w/ Russia = China

Nixon's arrival in the Soviet Union in May 1972, the first such visit by an American president since Roosevelt attended the Yalta summit 27 years earlier, came close on the heels of his much ballyhooed journey to China that February. The two trips were closely linked in Nixon's evolving grand strategy. Indeed, prior to the American president's China trip the Soviets had been dragging their feet in approving the SALT agreement; following Nixon's dramatic China foray, they acted with dispatch. Clearly, the Soviets did not want the Americans and Chinese to enter into a strategic partnership aimed against them; and, despite US protestations to the contrary, that was precisely what Nixon and Kissinger were seeking to do. It was the mounting Chinese fear of their Russian rivals that made a rapprochement with the once-hated Americans palatable to Mao and his top strategists. They, too, allowed geopolitical considerations to trump ideological convictions. 'The leaders of China were beyond ideology in their dealings with us', observed Kissinger. 'Their peril had established the absolute primacy of geopolitics.' Although little of a concrete nature emerged from Nixon's talks with Mao, Premier Zhou Enlai, and other Chinese officials, the symbolism of the trip proved extremely powerful. It seemed to herald a much less dangerous, less ideologically driven Cold War – and a much more diplomatically flexible and adroit United States.

The highlight and principal fruit of the Moscow meetings was SALT I, signed on 26 May 1972. It actually comprised two separate agreements. The first, a formal treaty, stipulated that the United States and the Soviet Union could each deploy ABMs at two, but only two, sites. The second part constituted an interim agreement on offensive nuclear weapons. It froze the existing number of ICBMs and SLBMs possessed by each signatory, granting the Soviets a 3-to-2 lead in the former and a slight edge in the latter. Since MIRVs were not prohibited nor long-range bombers restricted, however, the United States maintained a marked superiority in total, deliverable nuclear warheads, about 5,700 to 2,500. Nixon and Brezhnev also initialled a broad 'Basic Agreement' that laid out a code of conduct for the superpower relationship. Both sides agreed to 'do their utmost to avoid military confrontations and to prevent the outbreak of nuclear war', pledged 'restraint' in their relations with each other, and forswore 'efforts to obtain unilateral advantage at the expense of the other, directly or indirectly'. Although excessively vague and ultimately unenforceable, the guidelines served as a useful – and hopeful – set of behavioural benchmarks for each nation.

The value of the SALT accords derived more from the political significance of superpower negotiation and compromise than from the specific provisions contained in the individual agreements. 'SALT I did show that strategic arms limitation agreements could be negotiated', former diplomat and Soviet expert Raymond A. Garthoff has emphasized, 'notwithstanding the military, technical, security, political, and ideological differences between the two sides'. Yet his overall assessment contains some appropriate qualifications as well. Although SALT I 'did improve mutual understanding on at least some issues and for some time', it could not 'dispel all suspicions or prevent later massive strategic misunderstandings'. SALT I certainly did not halt the arms race. In fact, the interim agreement, which had a duration of five years, placed just a handful of limits on each side's nuclear arsenals, each of which continued to grow. A sharp spike in Soviet–American

10. Brezhnev and Nixon meeting during the Soviet leader's June 1973 visit to the United States.

trade, which grew from $220 million in 1971 to $2.8 billion in 1978, served as one of the more concrete by-products of detente. Along with projects for scientific cooperation, including a joint space probe and expanded cultural exchanges, the deepening trade links became one of the more prominent manifestations of the new Soviet–American relationship.

For those who longed for a genuine *reduction* in nuclear arms, hope lodged with future negotiations. Late in 1972, Soviet and American nuclear arms experts did open the next round of talks, dubbed SALT II. Disarray within the US Government, however, as the Watergate scandals first weakened Nixon and then forced his resignation in August 1974, militated against any appreciable progress. In November 1974, Gerald R. Ford, Nixon's successor, met with Brezhnev at Vladivostok to endorse a set of general principles to guide the SALT II negotiators. Yet no breakthrough appeared imminent, and the continuing negotiations were soon overshadowed by growing Congressional scepticism about the value

11. West German Chancellor Willy Brandt.

of the SALT process, mounting concern about Soviet actions in the Third World, and the upcoming US presidential election of 1976.

A process of European detente unfolded in parallel with the move towards superpower detente – and proved more durable. Willy Brandt, elected West German Chancellor in October 1969, assumed the lead role. A former mayor of West Berlin, the charismatic Brandt sought a gradual lowering of barriers to trade and travel between East and West Germany and a less exposed and vulnerable position for Germany in the Cold War. To achieve those goals, he was willing to recognize the *de facto* existence of the East German state, a significant departure from the standard position of the Federal Republic's political leaders. The first phase of Brandt's *Ostpolitik* concentrated on securing agreements with the Soviet Union and some of its Eastern European allies. In August 1970, West Germany signed a treaty with the Soviet Union in which each country renounced the use of force and pledged to respect Europe's existing boundaries as inviolable. Later that year, West Germany signed a similar agreement with Poland. A pact on Berlin followed. In September 1971, the Soviet Union, the United States, Great Britain, and France reached a quadripartite agreement that finally provided a legal sanction for the Western powers' rights within and access to West Berlin. The crowning achievement of Brandt's *Ostpolitik* came with the treaty between West and East Germany of December 1972. Each German entity recognized the legitimacy of the other, renounced the use of force, and pledged to increase trade and travel between east and west.

The process of European detente won popular acclaim on both sides of Europe's Cold War divide, leading to a significant increase in trade between Eastern and Western Europe, greater individual freedom of movement across the putative Iron Curtain, and a significant calming of tensions in central Europe. The easing of Cold War fears and barriers also facilitated movement towards a general European peace settlement. In November 1972, a preparatory Conference on Security and Cooperation in Europe

The Helsinki 'Final Act'

The accords reached at Helsinki comprised three distinct
elements, or 'baskets'. The first declared the inviolability of
existing European borders and enunciated the essential
principles that were to govern interstate relations. The
second covered economic, technological, scientific, and
environmental cooperation. 'Basket III', which the Soviet
Union had initially opposed, concerned basic human rights
within nations; it called for, among other matters, greater
freedom of speech and information and the freer movement
of people. The Soviet leadership went along with Basket III
as an acceptable, if distasteful, trade-off, so long as they were
simultaneously gaining the formal recognition of borders
and increased trade flows that they craved.

(CSCE) opened in Helsinki to prepare the groundwork for such a
settlement. Those discussions ultimately produced a 35-nation
gathering at the Finnish capital in July–August 1975, attended also
by the United States and the Soviet Union. The conferees accepted
the symbolic codification of the territorial changes imposed on
Europe after World War II, a goal long sought by Moscow.
The United States showed much less enthusiasm for the Helsinki
agreements, and for *Ostpolitik,* than did either the Europeans or
the Soviets. Former California Governor Ronald Reagan, a
presidential aspirant, said at the time: 'I think all Americans
should be against it.' What disturbed Reagan and other
conservative critics of the Helsinki Final Act – and the broader
process of detente from which it sprang – was the growing
tendency of the United States and other Western nations to
treat the Soviet Union more as a great power whose interests
needed to be accommodated than as an enemy state whose
unwavering quest for global domination remained a clear and

present danger. Developments in the Third World played into the hands of such critics.

Detente under siege

Detente never could live up to the high hopes engendered by the Moscow summit. The solemn pledges of the 'Basic Agreement' on superpower conduct failed to prevent the repeated clash of US and Soviet interests – in the Middle East, in Southeast Asia, in Africa, and elsewhere. Continuing Soviet–American conflict in the Third World, moreover, eroded support for detente within the United States. Conservative critics, many of whom had never tempered their ideological antipathy towards communism and their fundamental distrust of the Soviet state, charged that detente simply provided a cloak of legitimacy for Moscow's unaltered expansionist designs. A few even provocatively equated detente with appeasement. Technological advances further compounded the challenge faced by detente's proponents, since each advance rendered the achievement of balanced, verifiable, and mutually acceptable arms control agreements that much more elusive. In a bow to the swelling ranks of detente's opponents, President Ford, in 1976, actually banished the very word itself from the administration's vocabulary.

The Middle East War of October 1973 was one of the first major events to drive home detente's limitations. Anwar al-Sadat, who became Egypt's president following Nasser's death in 1970, worried that the thaw in superpower relations might block progress on his overriding policy goal of retrieving land lost to Israel in the disastrous 1967 war. In 1972, he expelled Soviet advisers from Egyptian soil, partly to register his disapproval with the shifting policy orientation of his principal patron. Then, on 16 October, Egypt and Syria launched a coordinated surprise attack against Israel in a bold effort to seize the military and diplomatic initiative. After initial battlefield setbacks, Israel soon recovered and gained the military upper hand. The Israeli counter-offensive was bolstered by the Nixon administration's decision to resupply equipment damaged or destroyed in the early fighting. That resupply effort intensified after the Soviet Union, for its part, began to resupply the Egyptians and Syrians. Though the mirror image of Washington's assistance to its long-term ally, Soviet actions appeared to Nixon as a dangerous threat – not just to Israel but also to detente. 'Our policy with respect to detente is clear,' Kissinger warned publicly. 'We shall resist aggressive foreign policies. Detente cannot survive irresponsibility in any area, including the Middle East.'

The international dimensions of the crisis precipitated by the third Arab–Israeli war were further widened by an Arab oil boycott of the United States in punishment for its pro-Israel policies, a move that struck directly at American economic self-interest.

The Middle East crisis took on more direct East–West overtones when Brezhnev called for the immediate deployment of a joint US–Soviet peacekeeping force, threatening unilateral Soviet action if necessary. The Russian leader, frustrated by Israel's failure to honour an agreed-upon cease-fire, and concerned that Egypt's surrounded army might be crushed by Israeli forces in the Sinai desert, made his appeal directly to Nixon. In the throes of the rapidly worsening Watergate scandal at the time, Nixon judged Brezhnev's gambit a major challenge to US interests in a vital, oil-rich region, and one that demanded a vigorous response. Consequently, he told the Soviet general secretary that the United States considered the prospect of unilateral Soviet action 'a matter of the gravest concern involving incalculable consequences'. To underscore his seriousness, Nixon placed US conventional and nuclear forces on worldwide alert, the first such alert since the height of the Cuban Missile Crisis. Diplomatic pressure on Israel to accept a cease-fire soon defused the crisis. By 27 October, the war was over, the US-led search for a peace settlement already entering into high gear. Yet the Soviet–American contretemps had definitely left its mark. If the Soviets and Americans could nearly come to blows over a regional dispute, what value did the Basic Agreement have? And, for all the high-minded rhetoric of government officials, how much closer had the world actually moved to the stable, peaceful international environment promised by detente's architects?

The final stages of the Vietnam War brought similar questions to the fore. Certainly detente offered no respite to America's travails in Indo-China. Nixon had hoped, initially, that rapprochement with both Moscow and Beijing might enable the United States to negotiate its way out of Vietnam with its honour and credibility intact. It had not worked that way. North Vietnamese negotiators proved unwilling to trim their long-sought political goals simply to meet the needs of a superpower in obvious retreat. The Nixon administration's periodic tactical escalations of the war similarly failed to break the negotiating logjam. Washington and Hanoi finally reached a peace settlement in January 1973, but while it allowed for the final withdrawal of US troops, the agreement brought no end to the fighting. In early 1975, North Vietnam launched an offensive against South Vietnam that led to the stunningly rapid collapse of a regime that over 58,000 Americans had died trying to protect from communism. The Ford administration's impotence in the Saigon government's final days, an impotence forced upon it by a Congress and public unwilling to countenance any additional commitments in Vietnam, certainly tarnished America's prestige as a global power. In subtle ways, too, the Vietnam debacle, with its searing images of a North Vietnamese invasion spearheaded by Soviet-made tanks, further exposed the limitations of superpower detente.

Developments in Angola, one of the more controversial and complex international flashpoints of the mid-1970s, wreaked additional damage on detente. Civil war among three competing factions broke out in the former Portuguese colony following Lisbon's grant of independence in November 1975. The involvement of Cuban troops on the side of the leftist Movement for the Popular Liberation of Angola (MPLA), which was battling more moderate, pro-Western factions backed covertly by the United States (and China), created a kind of proxy war in the West African territory. Kissinger, the consummate geopolitician, insisted that the Angolan conflict must be seen in East–West terms: as a test of will and resolve between Moscow and Washington, with weighty global implications. It was a test, he argued, from which the Soviet Union might draw unfortunate conclusions about the waning strength of a competitor that seemed substantially weakened by the cumulative impact of Nixon's forced resignation, defeat in Vietnam, and the ongoing Congressional assaults on the imperial presidency. Yet the Ford administration's appeal to Congress for stepped-up covert aid for its favoured Angolan factions failed. Legislators blanched at the notion of another Third World intervention so soon after Vietnam. Detente could not 'survive any more Angolas' warned Kissinger. Conservative critics of the Soviet–American thaw, for their part, found additional evidence in the Angolan affair to support their view that detente offered one-sided benefits to a still-expansionist Soviet Union.

The conservative assault on detente picked up steam throughout the mid- and late 1970s. It was mounted by a collection of well-placed intellectuals, journalists, politicians, and former government officials who shared little more than a deep-seated suspicion of Soviet intentions and a wariness about the Kremlin's evolving conventional and nuclear capabilities. Exhibit A for the anti-detentists was what seemed a continuing pattern of Soviet adventurism throughout the Third World. Exhibit B was what they claimed to be a deeply flawed process of arms control negotiations. Along with Democratic Senator Henry Jackson, Paul Nitze, an ardent anti-communist and former head of the State Department's Policy Planning Staff in the Truman administration, emerged as a leading spokesman for the anti-detentists. After resigning from the SALT II negotiating team, Nitze penned a stinging rebuke in the January 1976 issue of the influential journal *Foreign Affairs*. 'There is every prospect that under the terms of the SALT agreements the Soviet Union will continue to pursue a nuclear superiority that is not merely quantitative but designed to produce a theoretical war-winning capability,' he warned. 'If and only if the United States now takes action to redress the impending strategic imbalance can the Soviet Union be persuaded to abandon its quest for superiority and to resume the path of meaningful limitations and reductions through negotiation.'

The logic upon which this critique rested was rather dubious. Many nuclear specialists dismissed the notion that the Soviet Union was driving for nuclear superiority. They also disputed the related proposition that their heavier ICBMs might over time give the Soviets the ability to carry more nuclear warheads on their missiles, with greater 'throw weight', thereby permitting them to 'win' a nuclear confrontation with the United States. Kissinger responded to precisely such a doomsday scenario, as sketched by Nitze in testimony before Congress, with pained exasperation. 'What in the name of God *is* strategic superiority?', he implored. 'What is the significance of it, politically, militarily, operationally, at these levels of numbers? What do you do with it?' One suspects that behind the alarmism expressed by Nitze, Jackson, Reagan, and other critics of detente lay something other than the byzantine intricacies of counting overall nuclear warheads and measuring total throw weights. At a more fundamental level, these critics simply could not accept the very concepts of parity and sufficiency upon which detente was based. For diehard Cold Warriors, only strategic superiority – in every phase of nuclear and conventional weaponry – stood as an appropriate goal for the United States when dealing with so implacable and so inherently untrustworthy an adversary as the Soviet Union.

The election of Jimmy Carter imparted some fresh momentum to the beleaguered detente process, but it soon dissipated. The former governor of Georgia ran for the presidency as the candidate who would restore idealism to American foreign policy; he made human rights a key plank of his campaign and a central goal of his presidency. Yet Carter foundered, from the outset, in his dealings with the Soviet Union, pursuing contradictory goals and sending the Soviets conflicting signals. Only one month into his presidency, Carter wrote a warm letter to Andrei Sakharov, the renowned physicist and the Soviet Union's leading dissident – much to the discomfiture of the Kremlin hierarchy. Shortly thereafter, he sent his Secretary of State, Cyrus R. Vance, to Moscow with a poorly formulated proposal for making deeper cuts in offensive nuclear weapons than those previously worked out at the November 1974 meeting at Vladivostok. The new American president also signalled his intention to check the expanding Soviet involvement in Africa, as the political right within the United States was insisting. Yet in his first major foreign policy address, in May 1977, he declared that the time had come to move beyond the belief 'that Soviet expansion was almost inevitable but that it must be contained', beyond 'that inordinate fear of communism which once led us to embrace any dictator who joined us in that fear'. As historian John Lewis Gaddis has wryly pointed out, the Carter administration was trying 'to do everything at once: achieve a breakthrough on SALT, implement a human rights campaign, deter Moscow from seeking incremental shifts in the balance of power, and at the same time move away from the excessive preoccupation with the Soviet Union that had characterized Kissinger's diplomacy.' Yet, however worthy each of those goals might have been on its own terms, 'one could not simultaneously negotiate with, reform, deter, and ignore the Soviet Union.'

From the Kremlin's perspective, the new administration's approach to Soviet–American relations appeared at once confusing and threatening. Brezhnev denounced Carter's correspondence with the 'renegade' Sakharov, proclaiming that he would not 'allow interference in our internal affairs, whatever pseudo-humane pretense is used for the purpose'. Soviet policy-makers also cast a wary eye on Carter's proposal for more radical cuts in the already agreed upon SALT II arms control formula. Brezhnev considered it a 'personal affront', Ambassador Dobrynin a 'rude violation of our previous understanding'. As the latter subsequently remembered: 'We thought it wasn't serious, but an attempt to harass us, embarrass us.' Ever vigilant for any slights to their nation's status as a superpower of equal standing, Russian leaders worried that the United States was attempting to denigrate and delegitimize the Soviet state internationally while undermining it at home. Satisfied with the original framework of detente, they suspected Americans of seeking to overturn that framework in order to gain a strategic advantage.

Curiously, the ageing Kremlin rulers seemed incapable of grasping how provocative some of their actions appeared from Washington's perspective, or of recognizing how those actions were playing into the hands of detente's critics and thus speeding its demise. Soviet activism in Africa, Asia, and the Middle East certainly *was* of a much greater magnitude in the 1970s than in the past, a fact that Americans simply could not ignore. Flushed with its success in Angola, which led to the establishment of an MPLA government in February 1976, Moscow began supplying a new leftist regime in Ethiopia with arms the next year. In early 1978, Cuban troops, supplied and transported by the Soviets, routed US-backed Somali forces in fighting over the strategic Ogaden peninsula. The Soviets considered it not just their 'international duty' to 'assist the new revolutionary regimes which pledged their allegiance to socialism and the Soviet model', according to historian Odd Arne Westad, but also sensed 'an opportunity to hasten the internal contradictions and thereby the ultimate collapse of the capitalist world'. Reconciling such ambitions and actions with their parallel desire for productive, mutually beneficial relations with Washington, however, proved impossible.

Americans already sceptical of Moscow's intentions, such as Carter's National Security Adviser Zbigniew Brezinski, were convinced that they were witnessing a concerted geopolitical offensive against the West. The Brezhnev Politburo's decision to deploy new, intermediate-range nuclear missiles, the technologically sophisticated SS-20s, beginning in 1977, further discomfited American observers, as well as Western Europeans, whose cities they were targeted at. To regain the strategic initiative, the United States and its NATO partners began consideration of a counter-deployment of a new generation of American intermediate-range missiles in Europe. Brezinski also convinced Carter that it was time to play the 'China card'. The president agreed, moving to a formal opening of diplomatic ties with China on 1 January 1979, in large part to solidify a burgeoning strategic partnership with the Soviet Union's most feared rival and thus shore up the containment wall.

In the face of those mounting problems, on 18 June 1979, Carter and Brezhnev met in Vienna to sign the much-delayed SALT II agreement. The meeting was a subdued affair, possessing none of the soaring rhetoric of the Moscow summit seven years earlier. 'It was a mere instant of good feeling,' notes historian Gaddis Smith, 'evanescent as a soap bubble, the slightest of pauses in a deteriorating relationship.' Tension over Third World conflicts, the SS-20 deployments, America's human rights campaign, and deepening Sino–American ties had plainly taken their toll. Carter returned home to find the anti-detente forces in the ascendancy. Senator Jackson, from the opening bell of the ratification fight, registered his unequivocal opposition to SALT II. 'To enter a treaty which favors the Soviets as this one does on the ground that we will be in a worse position without it is appeasement in its purest form,' Jackson stormed. 'Against overwhelming evidence of a continuing Soviet strategic and conventional military buildup, there has been a flow of official administration explanations, extenuations, excuses.'

The overthrow of Nicaragua's authoritarian Anastasio Somoza Debayle, a longstanding US ally, by the Sandinistas, a Marxist-Leninist-led liberation movement with close ties to Cuba, further unsettled those who feared that anti-Western revolutionary forces were surging – as did events in Iran.

The Iranian Revolution and Hostage Crisis

In February 1979, an Islamic revolutionary movement, under the leadership of the Shi'ite religious leader Ayatollah Ruhollah Khomeini, gained power in Iran. Iran's new rulers viewed the United States with deep mistrust and suspicion, largely because it had been the principal backer of the Shah, the long-serving monarch they had despised and deposed. On 4 November 1979, shortly after the Shah was admitted into the United States for medical treatment, militants seized the US Embassy in Tehran, with the tacit support of Khomeini, and held 52 Americans hostage. The ensuing drama frustrated and humiliated Carter and the American people, contributing to the image of the United States as a nation in decline – a kind of impotent giant.

Then, at the end of December 1979, the Soviet Union invaded and occupied Afghanistan, sounding detente's final death knell. Carter phoned Brezhnev on the hot line and told him that the United States Government considered the Soviet invasion 'a clear threat to peace' which 'could mark a fundamental and long-lasting turning point in our relations'. The president told an interviewer that 'the action of the Soviets had made a more dramatic change in my opinion of what the Soviets' ultimate goals are than anything they've done in the previous time I've been in office'. The president responded to the Soviet move forcefully. He withdrew SALT II from Senate consideration, imposed economic sanctions on the Soviet Union, took a series of steps to reinvigorate containment, and called for a substantial increase in US defence spending. The Cold War was back – with a vengeance.

What killed detente? 'All in all', observed Soviet Ambassador Dobrynin in his memoirs, 'one could say that detente was to a certain extent buried in the fields of Soviet–American rivalry in the Third World.' It is difficult to dispute that assessment. The Soviets and Americans, from its inception, held different understandings of detente's meaning. For the Americans, it meant a Soviet Union bound to the existing world order; a Soviet Union that would act as a global stabilizing force. For the Russians, detente heralded their arrival and recognition as a co-equal power in a bipolar world, but did not preclude their continued support for revolutionary insurgencies and regimes across the Third World. In the mid-1960s, intelligence chief and future Soviet ruler Yuri Andropov forecast these tensions when he expressed the view that nothing should prevent the Soviets from exploiting the opportunities afforded them by any anti-capitalist, anti-Western movement. He predicted that 'the future competition with the United States will take place not in Europe, and not in the Atlantic Ocean. It will take place in Africa, and in Latin America.' And, Andropov insisted: 'We will compete for every piece of land, for every country.' That conception of detente proved incompatible with the conception popularized by Nixon and Kissinger of a new age of superpower cooperation. When added to the resurgence of conservative, virulently anti-communist political forces in the United States in the mid- and late 1970s, such fundamental incompatibilities ensured that the era of detente would be short-lived.

Chapter 8
The final phase, 1980–90

The late 1980s witnessed the most momentous changes in the
overall structure of world politics since the 1940s, culminating with
the sudden and wholly unexpected end of the ideological and
geopolitical struggle that had defined international relations for
45 years. Those remarkable developments occurred in a manner
and at a speed that almost no one expected, or even thought
possible. Why did the Cold War end when it did? How does one
make sense of a decade that opens with a rapidly intensifying Cold
War and closes with a historic Soviet-American rapprochement,
unprecedented arms control agreements, the withdrawal of
Soviet power from Eastern Europe, Afghanistan, and elsewhere,
and the peaceful reunification of Germany? This chapter
addresses those questions by examining the wild oscillations of
the Cold War's final phase.

Cold War redux

The Soviet invasion of Afghanistan completed Jimmy Carter's
improbable conversion to Cold War hardliner. Although the
Russians considered their military intervention a defensive action
aimed at preventing the emergence of a hostile regime on their
border, the president and most of his leading foreign policy experts
viewed it, instead, as part of a bold geopolitical offensive. They were
convinced that a confident, expansive-minded Soviet state was

vying to seize the strategic initiative from an America weakened by Vietnam, Watergate, the Iranian hostage crisis, and various economic shocks, with the ultimate goal of dominating the Persian Gulf region and denying its oil to the West. In response, Carter authorized a massive increase in US defence spending; he called for $1.2 trillion in military-related expenditures over the next five years. He also instituted a grain embargo against the Soviet Union, ordered a symbolic boycott of the 1980 summer Olympics scheduled to be held in Moscow, re-established military draft registration, and proclaimed a new 'Carter Doctrine' that promised to repel any effort by an outside power to gain control over the Persian Gulf 'by any means necessary, including military force'. The Carter administration applied additional pressure on the Soviets by strengthening the burgeoning US strategic partnership with China via the sale of advanced military hardware and technology. With vigorous American support, NATO also moved to implement a December 1979 decision to deploy new intermediate-range Pershing II and Cruise nuclear missiles in Western Europe to counter the Soviet SS-20s.

The Cold War mindset had returned to Washington policy circles with a vengeance, veritably burying any lingering memories of detente. 'Never since World War II has there been so far-reaching a militarization of thought and discourse in the capital,' observed an alarmed George F. Kennan in February 1980. 'An unsuspecting stranger, plunged into its midst, could only conclude that the last hope of peaceful, non-military solutions had been exhausted – that from now on only weapons, however used, could count.'

Ronald Reagan, who overwhelmed the vulnerable Carter in the November 1980 presidential election, certainly stood four-square with those who believed that only military strength mattered in the ongoing superpower competition. During the campaign, the former screen actor and California governor insisted that the United States must rebuild its defences in order to close a 'window of vulnerability' opened by the Soviet military build-up of the 1970s.

The most conservative and most ideological of America's post-World War II presidents, Reagan remained a diehard anti-communist with a visceral hatred for a regime that he considered as immoral as it was treacherous and untrustworthy. 'Let's not delude ourselves', Reagan declared during one campaign stop. 'The Soviet Union underlies all the unrest that is going on. If they weren't engaged in this game of dominoes, there wouldn't be any hot spots in the world.' He rejected out of hand the treat-the-Soviet-Union-as-an-ordinary-power ethos of the Nixon, Ford, and early Carter years. At his very first presidential press conference, Reagan set the tone for his first term by accusing Moscow of using detente as 'a one-way street . . . to pursue its own aims', including 'the promotion of world revolution and a one-world Socialist or Communist state'. Soviet leaders, the new American chief executive charged, 'reserve unto themselves the right to commit any crime, to lie, to cheat, in order to attain that'.

Such inflammatory rhetoric became a hallmark of the renewed Cold War waged by the Reagan administration. Along with a huge military build-up and a concerted effort to roll back Soviet power through increased support and encouragement for anti-communist insurgencies across the globe, it constituted a central element of America's reinvigorated containment strategy. Employing language that hearkened back to the Truman years, Reagan regularly berated both the Soviet state and the ideology that undergirded it. In 1982, he confidently proclaimed in a speech to the British Parliament that Marxism-Leninism was doomed 'to the ash heap of history'. The next year, before the National Association of Evangelicals, in Orlando, Florida, Reagan described the Soviet Union as 'the focus of evil in the modern world'. He implored his audience to resist 'the aggressive impulses of an evil Empire', emphasizing that the struggle against communism was at root a moral one 'between right and wrong and good and evil'. That Manichean reformulation of the Cold War as a righteous battle between the forces of light and the forces of darkness suggested that no quarter could be given, no detente era compromises risked.

Reagan was determined to expand the nation's nuclear and conventional military capabilities before engaging in any serious negotiations with the Soviets. 'Peace through strength' became a favourite catchphrase of the president and his defence planners; that oft-repeated slogan also served to rationalize the administration's initially desultory approach to arms control negotiations. Despite ample evidence to the contrary, the Republican president and his top foreign policy advisers were convinced that, over the previous decade, American power had declined relative to that of the Soviet Union. Alexander M. Haig, Jr, Reagan's first secretary of state, claimed that when he assumed office in January 1981 the Soviet Union 'possessed greater military power than the United States, which had gone into a truly alarming military decline even before the withdrawal from Vietnam accelerated the weakening trend.'

To reverse that supposed weakening trend, Reagan set a five-year defence spending target of $1.6 trillion, more than $400 billion over the already substantial increase projected by Carter during his final year in the White House. It was the largest peacetime arms build-up in US history. 'Defense is not a budget item', Reagan told the Pentagon. 'Spend what you need.' Among other priorities, he revived the expensive B-1 bomber programme, approved development of the B-2 (Stealth) bomber, accelerated deployment of the controversial MX (Missile Experimental) and the sophisticated Trident submarine missile system, expanded the Navy from 450 to 600 ships, and pumped substantial new funds into the CIA to support an enhanced covert arm. Although Reagan presented his military expansion as a drive simply to regain America's 'margin of safety', it actually represented a bid to re-establish US strategic superiority – a status that Reagan and many fellow conservatives had never been willing to surrender in the first place.

Not surprisingly, Russia's rulers grew progressively more alarmed at the belligerent rhetoric and assertive behaviour of the most hostile US administration they had faced in at least two decades. Just as vigilant as the Americans in gauging both the capabilities and intentions of their principal adversary, Soviet defence officials worried that the United States might be seeking to develop the potential for a devastating first strike against Soviet missile silos and industrial centres. Those suspicions multiplied after Reagan's unveiling of his Strategic Defense Initiative in March 1983. The president announced in a public speech that he was ordering 'a comprehensive and intensive effort' to 'search for ways to reduce the danger of nuclear war' through the development of a defensive missile shield. Reagan sketched a Utopian vision of a future free from nuclear danger: 'What if free people could live secure in the knowledge that their security did not rest upon the threat of instant U.S. retaliation to deter a Soviet attack, that we could intercept and destroy strategic ballistic missiles before they reached our own soil or that of our allies?'

Most experts considered a comprehensive missile shield technologically unfeasible. Nonetheless, the surprise initiative raised the spectre of more limited defensive systems that could eventually render the prevailing structure of mutual deterrence null and void, thereby destabilizing the Soviet-American strategic balance. No less an expert than former Secretary of Defense McNamara observed that the Soviets could be forgiven for believing that with SDI the United States was seeking a first strike capability. That is precisely what some did believe. Yuri Andropov, who became the Soviet leader after the death of Brezhnev in November 1982, exclaimed that the Reagan administration was embarking on 'an extremely dangerous path'. The former KGB chief condemned SDI as 'a bid to disarm the Soviet Union in the face of the U.S. nuclear threat'.

During the second half of 1983, US–Soviet relations reached a nadir. On 1 September 1983, Soviet air defences shot down a Korean civilian airliner en route from Anchorage, Alaska, that had inadvertently strayed into Russian airspace, killing all 269 passengers, including 61 Americans. The next day, Reagan went on national television to denounce what he termed the 'Korean airline massacre' as a completely unjustified 'crime against humanity'. He called it 'an act of barbarism, born of a society which wantonly disregards individual rights and the value of human life'. Unwarranted Soviet suspicions that the plane had been on an espionage mission and their failure to show much remorse for the tragic episode combined with the Reagan administration's rhetorical overreaction to heighten tensions further. Andropov, in rapidly failing health at the time, complained about the 'outrageous militarist psychosis' prevalent in Washington. Then, in early November, NATO went ahead with a scheduled military exercise that so frightened Soviet intelligence specialists they suspected it might be a prelude to, and cover for, a full-scale nuclear strike against the Soviet Union. The Kremlin ordered a military alert, and US intelligence learned that nuclear-capable aircraft had been placed on stand-by at East German air bases. Soviet leaders had truly come to believe the Reagan administration capable of undertaking a pre-emptive nuclear war. In December, Soviet representatives withdrew from the ongoing, if largely unproductive, arms control negotiations at Geneva. They were protesting the recent deployment of the initial batch of US Pershing II and Cruise missiles in Western Europe. For the first time in 15 years, US and Soviet negotiators were no longer even talking to each other in any forum.

Yet for all its rhetorical and budgetary bluster, the Reagan administration took pains to avoid any direct military confrontation with the Soviet Union. The only major deployment of US armed forces against what was identified as a Soviet client state took place in tiny Grenada, in October 1983. The United States mounted a 7,000-man invasion force to topple an indigenous Marxist regime that had recently gained power in that Caribbean island via a

12. Afghan mujaheddin rebels with captured Soviet weapons, near Matun, 1979.

bloody coup, and to save in the process several dozen supposedly endangered American medical students. US troops overwhelmed Grenada's 600-man army and 636 Cuban construction workers – to clamorous public acclaim throughout the United States. More characteristic of Reagan's approach, however, and of much greater significance to his Cold War strategy, was the stepped-up provision of assistance, often of a covert nature, to anti-communist guerrillas battling against Soviet-supported regimes throughout the Third World. In what came to be called the Reagan Doctrine, the United States vied to roll back Soviet power on the periphery through the use of indigenous, anti-leftist insurgents as proxy warriors – principally in Afghanistan, Nicaragua, Angola, and Cambodia. In his January 1985 state-of-the-union address Reagan proclaimed: 'We must not break faith with those who are risking their lives – on every continent, from Afghanistan to Nicaragua – to defy Soviet-supported aggression.' Yet, grandiloquent rhetoric aside, one of the most telling aspects of the American effort to challenge Soviet-backed governments in the Third World was the administration's reluctance in so doing to risk either the lives of regular US military personnel or the possibility of a direct clash with the Soviet Union.

Countervailing pressures

The Reagan administration's aggressive approach to the Cold War met with opposition not just from an unnerved Soviet ruling circle but from within the West as well. Key NATO allies recoiled from what some saw as an overly belligerent, and excessively dangerous, American stance. 'The first half of the 1980s saw a recurrent pattern' notes historian David Reynolds – 'the United States at odds with the Soviets *and* with its European allies as well'. Public opinion within Western Europe, and within the United States itself, registered deep unease about the sure-to-be catastrophic consequences of a nuclear war that suddenly appeared less unthinkable than it had been for nearly a generation. Allied and public pressure exerted powerful countervailing pressures on the

Reagan administration, pushing it back to the negotiating table by mid-decade, even before the advent of the Mikhail Gorbachev regime provided it with an eager and compliant negotiating partner.

Discord within the Atlantic alliance was nothing new, of course. Inter-allied disputes had wracked NATO since its earliest days – over decolonization, Suez, Vietnam, defence-sharing, and numerous issues of broad Cold War strategy. Yet the intensity of the clashes between the United States and its European partners reached unprecedented proportions during Reagan's first term in office. Poland served as one especially nettlesome source of conflict. In December 1981, the Soviet-backed government of General Wojciech Jaruzelski imposed martial law on its restive citizens, cracking down on the independent, non-communist labour union *Solidarity*. America's European allies resisted Reagan's vigorous push for broad-based sanctions against Moscow as punishment for unleashing 'the forces of tyranny' against Poland. They confined themselves to a modest ban on new credits to the Warsaw government. Hardliners in the Reagan administration fumed; they privately castigated the Europeans as unprincipled appeasers who were unwilling to take any action that might jeopardize lucrative trade links with the Eastern bloc. To force the issue, the administration used the Polish crackdown as a pretext for subverting a planned natural gas pipeline deal between the Soviet Union and several Western European countries, thereby precipitating a far more serious European–American clash of interests.

Following West Germany's lead, several European countries had agreed to help construct a 3,500-mile pipeline that would connect Siberia's vast natural gas fields to Western European markets. The mammoth $15 billion pipeline project would lessen European dependence on energy resources from the unstable Middle East while strengthening East–West trade links and providing needed jobs to a Europe mired in recession. Worried that the pipeline might lead some of its closest allies to become too reliant economically on the Soviet Union and hence vulnerable to a form of economic blackmail, Reagan announced a prohibition on the sale of US pipeline technology to the Soviet Union within weeks of Poland's martial law proclamation. In June 1982, the president applied even stronger pressure, ordering that any European firms utilizing US-licensed technology or equipment as well as any American subsidiaries operating in Europe must revoke all contracts for pipeline-related work. The abrupt US action infuriated European leaders. The French foreign minister charged that the United States had declared 'economic warfare on her allies' and warned that this could be 'the beginning of the end of the Atlantic Alliance'. With characteristic bluntness, West German Chancellor Helmut Schmidt snapped: 'For all practical purposes, U.S. policy has taken on a form that suggests an end to friendship and partnership.' Even British Prime Minister Margaret Thatcher, America's most loyal ally and Europe's most anti-Soviet political leader, was outraged by Reagan's heavy-handedness. 'The question is whether one very powerful nation can prevent existing contracts from being fulfilled', she observed. 'I think it is wrong to do that.'

In the face of those vigorous protests, the Reagan administration backed off. In November 1982, after six months of testy negotiations, it jettisoned its policy of sanctions. The episode drove home to policy-makers in Washington the deep reluctance of Western Europeans to tear the fabric of the Euro-Soviet detente that had proven both popular and economically beneficial. Although Soviet–American detente had unravelled at the end of the 1970s, its European variant maintained its momentum. By the early 1980s, close to half a million West German jobs were tied to trade with the East; the pipeline deal, moreover, seemed a godsend to energy-dependent Western Europeans. Why renounce lucrative commercial transactions with the Soviet bloc, asked European diplomats, politicians, and businessmen, just to placate an ally that had itself recently resumed grain sales to the Soviet Union to honour a campaign promise made by Reagan to American farmers? US hypocrisy grated on European sensibilities nearly as much as US arrogance. And, in a still broader sense, European defence planners did not see the Soviet threat in the same apocalyptic terms as did their colleagues across the Atlantic.

The deployment of a new generation of US intermediate-range nuclear missiles in Western Europe proved the most contentious trans-Atlantic issue of all. It pitted not only the United States against certain European governments, but also pitted some of those same governments against their own people. The problem originated in 1977 with the Soviet deployment of its mobile, land-based SS-20s in European Russia, most of which were targeted at Germany. The Carter administration at first proposed countering the new Soviet deployment with an enhanced radiation weapon, termed the neutron bomb. When Carter decided, in 1978, not to deploy the controversial neutron bomb, he angered Chancellor Schmidt who was already grumbling about American unreliability. NATO's decision, just two weeks before the Soviet invasion of Afghanistan, to dispatch 572 Pershing II and Cruise missiles to Germany, Great Britain, Italy, Belgium, and the Netherlands grew out of the neutron bomb fiasco. Yet the decision was a contingent one since it was coupled with a commitment to press ahead simultaneously with new arms control talks with the Soviets aimed at achieving a stable balance of theatre nuclear weapons in Europe – the so-called 'dual track'. If successful, or so many Europeans hoped, those talks might foreclose the need to follow through with the promised US deployments. Upon assuming power, Reagan vowed to move forward expeditiously with the intermediate nuclear force (INF) deployments, but his publicly expressed disdain for arms control agreements meant that the continuing talks with the Soviets would almost certainly go nowhere.

The prospect of new US nuclear weapons on European soil, in conjunction with the pronounced chill in Soviet–American relations and the overheated anti-communist rhetoric emanating from the White House, prompted the deepest level of public concern about the nuclear arms race in decades. The imminent introduction of the Pershing II and Cruise missiles, as a result, helped trigger a massive, broad-based peace movement throughout Western Europe. In West Germany, the 'Krefeld Appeal' of November 1980, advanced by major religious and political groups, soon gained over 2.5 million signatures in support of its central plank: 'atomic death threatens us all – no atomic weapons in Europe'. In October 1981, millions of Europeans joined mass protest rallies against American – and Soviet – missile deployments. Bonn, London, and Rome hosted rallies that each attracted over 250,000 demonstrators. The next month, 500,000 marched in Amsterdam in the biggest mass protest in Dutch history. Reagan had unwittingly added fuel to the fire when, just prior to the peace marches, he responded to a reporter's question by commenting that a battlefield exchange of nuclear weapons could occur without 'it bringing either one of the major powers to push the button'. The remark garnered sensational headlines in Europe – since Europe would of course be the 'battlefield' to which Reagan so casually alluded. When the American president visited France and West Germany in June 1982, he was greeted with more mass demonstrations, including a peaceful gathering of 350,000 anti-nuclear protestors along the banks of the Rhine River in Bonn and a boisterous crowd of over 100,000 in West Berlin. The latter assemblage gathered in defiance of a ban imposed against all demonstrations during the Reagan visit, touching off a major riot. In October 1983, several million more Europeans took to the streets of London, Rome, Bonn, Hamburg, Vienna, Brussels, The Hague, Stockholm, Paris, Dublin, Copenhagen, and other major cities in an impressive, albeit unsuccessful, final effort to block the INF deployments.

The European peace movement enjoyed broad support. From early 1983 onwards, the two leading opposition political parties in Great Britain and West Germany – Labour and the Social Democrats – came out against the Pershing II and Cruise missiles. Trade union,

14. Anti-nuclear demonstrators in Brussels carry a mock effigy of President Reagan, October 1981.

church, and student groups throughout Western Europe also gravitated to the anti-nuclear cause. According to a 1982 poll, approval of the peace movement in the major NATO countries ranged from a low of 55% to a high of 81%. After reviewing the poll data, chief US arms negotiator Paul Nitze admitted at a State Department meeting: 'We have a political problem in Europe.'

The Reagan administration faced a political problem at home as well, where growing public consciousness about the danger of nuclear war gave rise to the largest peace coalition since the Vietnam War. As in Western Europe, the churches proved instrumental to the movement. The influential World Council of Churches advocated a halt to the nuclear arms race, as did the ordinarily apolitical Roman Catholic Bishops of the United States. In a 150-page pastoral letter of May 1983, the Catholic Bishops stressed: 'We are the first generation since Genesis with the power to virtually destroy God's creation.' They also proclaimed, in a direct repudiation of administration policy, that 'the quest for nuclear superiority must be rejected'. Medical and scientific voices joined the debate, emphasizing the calamitous human consequences of nuclear war. Some scientists talked of a 'nuclear winter' that would follow any major nuclear conflict, disastrously cooling the earth's temperature to the extent that much plant and animal life would be extinguished. To illustrate the impact upon a typical American city, Physicians for Social Responsibility publicized what a one-megaton nuclear bomb hitting central Boston would mean: more than 2 million deaths, with the downtown area obliterated, and the surrounding suburbs reeling from the explosion and its accompanying radiation effects. The *Detroit Free Press* superimposed a target over Detroit in a Sunday magazine supplement, with a related story about the frightening levels of death and devastation that a nuclear attack would visit on that city. Jonathan Schell's best-selling book *The Fate of the Earth* (1982) contained compendious, grisly details about the aftermath of nuclear war. And, most influential of all, ABC television broadcast 'The Day After', a show watched by 100 million Americans that

15. Anti-nuclear demonstration in New York City, 12 June 1982.

vividly dramatized the aftermath of a nuclear attack in the city of Lawrence, Kansas. Reagan was sufficiently alarmed about the cultural impact of 'The Day After' that he had Secretary of State George P. Shultz appear on ABC immediately afterwards in an effort to help modulate the public reaction.

The nuclear freeze movement, which peaked between 1982 and 1984, served as the chief political fruit of the growing anti-nuclear consciousness among the American populace. A 12 June 1982 demonstration in New York's Central Park drew close to one million people in support of a freeze on each of the superpowers' nuclear arsenals. It still ranks as the largest political demonstration in the nation's history. The movement garnered strong support within the Congress as well. On 4 May 1983, in fact, the House of Representatives approved a nuclear freeze resolution by the decisive vote of 278 to 149. Public opinion polls registered approval ratings of no less than 70% for the nuclear freeze movement throughout these years. Polls also offer some of the strongest evidence for the general public unease with the military policies of the Reagan administration. According to one poll, 50% of a representative sample of American citizens believed that the nation would be safer if its leaders spent more time negotiating with the Soviets and less time building up military forces; only 22% disagreed. Similarly, a Gallup poll of December 1983 reported that 47% of Americans believed that the Reagan military build-up had brought the United States 'closer to war' rather than 'closer to peace', whereas only 28% disagreed.

In response to those political realities, Reagan deliberately softened his rhetoric as 1984 began. Some of his closest political advisers had persuaded the president that foreign policy issues loomed as his greatest potential liability with American voters in that year's presidential election and that a more conciliatory approach towards the Soviet Union would strengthen his bid for re-election. Secretary of State Shultz was also pushing strongly for re-engagement with the Russians. Consequently, in an important speech that January,

Beware the bear

One of the most memorable television advertisements run by the Reagan campaign during the 1984 election featured a large, menacing brown bear. As the bear crashed through a forest, the narrator solemnly explained: 'There is a bear in the woods. For some people, the bear is easy to see. Others don't see it at all. Some people say the bear is tame. Others say it's vicious, and dangerous. Since no one can really be sure who's right, isn't it smart to be as strong as the bear – if there is a bear?' The allegorical commercial was intended, quite obviously, to remind voters that Reagan remained unwilling to risk the nation's security by dropping its guard at a time when the unpredictable Russian bear was still on the prowl.

Reagan offered an olive branch to Moscow, calling 1984 'a year of opportunities for peace' and declaring a willingness to renew negotiations. In the peroration to that speech, drafted by Reagan himself, the president sketched a vivid portrait of two ordinary American and Soviet couples – 'Jim and Sally' and 'Ivan and Anya' – who each longed for peace between their respective countries. On 24 September, in the midst of the election campaign, Reagan proposed before the UN General Assembly that a new Soviet—American negotiating framework be established that would combine under one umbrella three different nuclear arms talks: on intermediate nuclear forces (INF), on strategic arms limitations (START), and on anti-satellite weapons (ASAT).

Shortly after Reagan's resounding re-election in November, Moscow agreed to participate in negotiations under that framework. Constantin Chernenko, who had ascended to the position of first secretary of the Communist Party in February 1984, after Andropov's death, approved the commencement of the new talks. They began in March 1985, but quickly bogged down; the main obstacle to progress proved Reagan's coveted missile defence programme, an initiative the Soviets still considered dangerously destabilizing. The opening of the talks happened to coincide with an internal Soviet development of far greater import for the future: the replacement of the sickly Chernenko, after just over one year in power, with a dramatically different type of Soviet leader.

Gorbachev and the end of the Cold War

The accession, in March 1985, of Mikhail S. Gorbachev to the position of general secretary of the Soviet Communist Party stands as the most critical turning point in the Cold War's final phase – the one factor, above all others, that hastened the end of the Cold War and the radical transformation in Soviet–American relations that accompanied it. The dynamic, 54-year-old Gorbachev made virtually all of the major concessions that led to landmark arms reduction agreements in the late 1980s. Through a series of wholly unexpected, often unilateral, overtures and concessions, he succeeded in changing the entire tenor of the Soviet–American relationship, in the end depriving the United States of the enemy whose presumably expansionist designs it had been seeking to thwart for the past 45 years. Absent this remarkable individual, the astonishing changes of the 1985–90 period become nearly inconceivable.

Gorbachev and his foreign minister, Eduard Shevadrnadze, advanced dramatic new ideas about security, nuclear weapons, and the relationship of both to their highest priorities: domestic reform and the revitalization of socialism. Influenced by a changing intellectual milieu in the Soviet Union, shaped in part by Soviet scientists and foreign policy experts with broad exposure to the West and close contact with their Western counterparts, Gorbachev and Shevardnadze injected 'new thinking' into both the staid Kremlin leadership circle and the stalled Soviet–American dialogue. 'My impression is that he's really decided to end the arms race no matter what', Gorbachev's aide Anatoly Chernayev noted about his boss in early 1986: 'He is taking this 'risk' because, as he understands, it's no risk at all because nobody would attack us even if we disarmed completely. And in order to get the country out on solid ground, we have to relieve it of the burden of the arms race, which is a drain on more than just the economy.'*

Gorbachev and Shevardnadze had reached the conclusion that the arms race was self-defeating; it added nothing to the nation's real security while burdening an already strapped economy. 'Traditional centuries-old notions of national security as the defense of the country from external military threat have been shaken by profound structural and qualitative shifts in human civilization,' insisted Shevardnadze, 'the result of the growing role of science and technology and the increasing political, economic, social, and information interdependence of the world.'

True security, Gorbachev asserted, could only be provided 'by political means', not military means. Global 'interdependence', he emphasized, 'is such that all peoples are similar to climbers roped together on the mountainside. They either can climb together to the summit or fall together into the abyss.' Any 'striving for military superiority', he commented on another occasion, 'means chasing one's own tail.' Convinced that no rational person or state would use nuclear weapons, and that the Soviet Union possessed at any rate a sufficient nuclear arsenal for national self-protection, the new leaders thought the overarching goal of Soviet foreign policy should be to encourage a joint nuclear, and conventional, arms build-down with the United States. Doing so, they believed, would simultaneously foster a safer and more secure international environment and free up resources needed for long-overdue internal reforms of their deeply troubled economic system. Gorbachev's domestic push for *perestroika* (restructuring) and *glasnost* (openness) was thus intimately linked from the first with his determination to halt the arms race with the United States and to bring an abrupt end to the relationship of poisonous hostility that had developed between the superpowers since the end of detente.

The rapid-fire series of events that transpired between 1985 and 1990 stunned governmental decision-makers, foreign policy experts, and ordinary citizens alike across the world. Yet those epochal events, it is now evident, were preceded and conditioned by the new thinking about security, nuclear weapons, and domestic needs that animated all of Gorbachev's dealings with the United States, Eastern Europe, and the world at large. Ronald Reagan, the most unequivocally anti-communist American leader of the entire Cold War era, suddenly found a Soviet leader saying yes to arms control faster than he could say no, moving to 'deideologize' Moscow's foreign policy, offering unilateral concessions on conventional armed forces, and vowing to remove Soviet troops from Afghanistan. To his great credit, Reagan proved willing first to moderate, and then to abandon, deeply held personal convictions about the malignant nature of communism, thereby permitting a genuine rapprochement to occur.

The two men met five separate times between 1985 and 1988, developing a stronger rapport with each summit. After a get-acquainted summit at Geneva in November 1985 that produced little of substance but markedly improved the atmospherics of the Soviet–American relationship, Gorbachev convinced Reagan to attend a hastily arranged meeting at Reykjavik, Iceland, in October 1986. There, the two leaders came remarkably close to a decision to eliminate all ballistic missiles. In the end, though, Reagan's insistence on continuing with his SDI initiative led the Soviet leader to withdraw the breathtaking proposals he had placed on the table. Yet the setback at Reykjavik proved but temporary. Shortly thereafter, Gorbachev dropped his insistence that America's abandonment of SDI must be a prerequisite for progress on all arms control matters, and moved to accept the 'zero option' first put forward by US negotiators back in 1981 – and then largely as a propaganda ploy since it so plainly favoured the American side.

Gorbachev's concessions led to the conclusion of the Intermediate Nuclear Forces Treaty, signed at the December 1987 Washington summit. Reagan, in his public remarks, jocularly repeated what he called an old Russian maxim: '*doveryai no proveryai* – trust, but verify'. The Soviet ruler offered a more soaring vision. 'May December 8, 1987, become a date that will be inscribed in the history books,' he declared, 'a date that will mark the watershed separating the era of a mounting risk of nuclear war from the era of a demilitarization of human life.' The INF Treaty, rapidly ratified by the US Senate, led to the destruction of 1,846 Soviet nuclear weapons and 846 US weapons within three years, with each side allowing close, and unprecedented, inspection of the other side's nuclear sites. For the first time in the atomic era, an actual class of nuclear weapons was being not just limited but eliminated.

Reagan's trip to Moscow in the spring of 1988 testified even more powerfully to the ongoing transformation in Soviet–American relations – and the Cold War. The leaders of the two superpowers were now plainly treating each other more as friendly partners than as enemies. The American president even disavowed his previous depiction of the Soviet state as an evil empire. When asked by a reporter if he still thought of the Soviet Union in such terms, Reagan replied: 'No. I was talking about another time, another era.' In his public comments before departing Moscow, the man who had issued some of the harshest denunciations of the Soviet state since the Cold War's inception asked Gorbachev to 'tell the people of the Soviet Union of the deep feelings of friendship' that he, his wife Nancy, and the American people had towards them. He expressed 'hope for a new era in human history, an era of peace between our nations and peoples'. Certainly the images of Reagan and Gorbachev amiably strolling arm-in-arm across Red Square and the American president speaking with his trademark avuncular charm to students at Moscow State University, in front of a huge bust of Lenin no less, spoke volumes about the remarkable metamorphosis that had taken place.

13. Reagan and Gorbachev stroll together in Moscow's Red Square
during Reagan's May 1988 visit to Moscow.

In December 1988, Gorbachev made another visit to the United States to meet with Reagan, one last time, while also conducting discussions with – and sizing up – president-elect George Bush. That trip coincided with a major speech the Soviet leader delivered at the United Nations, in which he revealed his intention to reduce unilaterally Soviet military forces by 500,000 troops. 'Perhaps not since Woodrow Wilson presented his Fourteen Points in 1918 or since Franklin Roosevelt and Winston Churchill promulgated the Atlantic Charter in 1941', gushed the *New York Times* in a lead editorial, 'has a world figure demonstrated the vision Mikhail Gorbachev displayed yesterday at the United Nations.'

Gorbachev's proposal led to a significant reduction of the Soviet military presence in Eastern Europe. It also signalled, as did a series of his public and private statements, that the Kremlin leadership was discarding the so-called Brezhnev Doctrine – the notion that the Soviet Union would use force, if necessary, to maintain rigid control over each of its Warsaw Pact allies. With the loosening of the Soviet grip, Eastern European dissidents exulted, old-line communist *apparatchiks* quaked. What followed with remarkable speed were popular democratic revolutions that swept out of power every communist regime in Eastern Europe, beginning with Poland in mid-1989, where the once-banned *Solidarity* formed a new government, and ending with the violent denouement of the Nikolae Ceausescu regime in Romania at year's close. The event that most powerfully symbolized the crumbling of the old order was the opening of the Berlin Wall on 9 November. That infamous 28-mile-long concrete barrier had come to signify not just the division of Germany's former capital, but the division of Europe as a whole. As the wall disintegrated, so too did Europe's East–West divide. 'The total dismantling of socialism as a world phenomenon has been proceeding', Anatoly Chernayev wrote in his diary. 'And a common fellow from Stavropol set this process in motion.' To the delight of the Bush administration, which wisely chose not to exult at the repudiation of Eastern Europe's communist states,

Gorbachev – that common fellow from Stavropol – simply let events run their course.

In many respects, the demolition of the Berlin Wall and the concomitant implosion not just of Eastern Europe's communist governments but of the entire Warsaw Pact alliance system meant the end of the Cold War. The ideological contest was now over. Neither communism nor the Soviet state any longer posed a serious threat to the security of the United States or its allies. Many observers have, accordingly, cited 1989 as the Cold War's terminal date. Yet, at that point, one crucial issue remained unresolved: the status of Germany. It was the very issue, moreover, whose importance and intractability first precipitated the Soviet–American breach in the immediate aftermath of World War II.

Chancellor Helmut Kohl's West German government began pressing for reunification once the wall came down, presenting the Kremlin with a daunting strategic dilemma. Gorbachev had calculated that Soviet security no longer demanded the preservation of compliant, satellite regimes in Eastern Europe. But Germany was different. A divided Germany had formed a core element of Soviet security policy ever since Stalin's reign. 'We had paid an enormous price for it', noted Shevardnadze, 'and to write it off was inconceivable. The memory of the war was stronger than the new concepts about the limits of security.' In the end, though, Gorbachev accepted by mid-1990 the inevitability of a reunified Germany. Unwilling to use force to thwart what seemed the near irresistible momentum towards unity, the Soviet leader took solace in Bush's assurances that Germany would remain enmeshed in the Western security system. Gorbachev's greatest fear was of an unharnessed, newly empowered Germany becoming a future menace to Russian security – the exact same fear, it bears emphasizing, that lay behind Stalin's approach to the German problem during and right after World War II. The record of over four decades of German democracy, however, served to dilute those fears. Coupled with the American insistence that Germany would

16. The Berlin Wall comes down, November 1989.

remain locked into, rather than independent from, NATO, that record of peace, stability, and democratic governance helped assuage Gorbachev's anxieties.

By the summer of 1990, the Soviets, Americans, British, French, and Germans agreed that the two Germanies would henceforth constitute a single, sovereign country that would remain anchored to the NATO alliance. With German power now fully co-opted in the Western coalition, one of the greatest Cold War worries of US officialdom – that of a unified, pro-Soviet Germany – disappeared. The succinct observation of Brent Scowcroft, Bush's National Security Adviser, that 'the Cold War ended when the Soviets accepted a united Germany in NATO' thus seems essentially correct. The year 1990, rather than 1989, truly marked the end of the Cold War. The collapse of the Soviet Union itself in 1991, the product of forces set in motion by Gorbachev's reforms that he proved unable to control, stands as a critically important historical event in its own right, but an anti-climactic one insofar as the Cold War is concerned. By the time the Soviet Union disappeared, the Cold War itself was already history.

---

* This and several of the following quotes, along with much of the line of analysis presented in this section, are drawn from an unpublished essay by Melvyn P. Leffler, "The Beginning and the End: Time, Context, and the Cold War," in *The Cold War in the 1980's*, ed. Olav Njolstad (London, forthcoming).

Further reading

A number of books ably cover the entirety of the Cold War. Particularly recommended are David S. Painter, *The Cold War: An International History* (London, 1999); Martin Walker, *The Cold War: A History* (London, 1993); S. J. Ball, *The Cold War: An International History, 1947–1991* (London, 1998); Richard J. Crockatt, *The Fifty Years War: The United States and the Soviet Union in World Politics, 1941–1991* (London, 1995); Walter LaFeber, *America, Russia, and the Cold War, 1945–2000*, 9th edn. (New York, 2002); Ronald E. Powaski, *The Cold War: The United States and the Soviet Union, 1917–1991* (New York, 1998); Geoffrey Roberts, *The Soviet Union in World Politics: Coexistence, Revolution and Cold War, 1945–1991* (London, 1999); Thomas J. McCormick, *America's Half-Century: United States Foreign Policy in the Cold War* (Baltimore, 1989); Warren I. Cohen, *America in the Age of Soviet Power, 1945–1991* (New York, 1993); and H. W. Brands, *The Devil We Knew: Americans and the Cold War* (New York, 1993).

Important works that utilize new archival sources to reinterpret the first half of the Cold War include Vladislav Zubok and Constantine Pleshakov, *Inside the Kremlin's Cold War: From Stalin to Khrushchev* (Cambridge, Mass., 1996) and John Lewis Gaddis, *We Now Know: Rethinking Cold War History* (Oxford, 1997). A useful collection is Odd Arne Westad (ed.), *Reviewing the Cold War: Approaches, Interpretations, Theory* (London, 2000).

Chapter 1

Melvyn P. Leffler, *The Specter of Communism: The United States and the Origins of the Cold War, 1917–1953* (New York, 1994).

Vojtech Mastny, *The Cold War and Soviet Insecurity: The Stalin Years* (New York, 1996).

Williamson Murray and Allan R. Millett, *A War To Be Won: Fighting the Second World War* (Cambridge, Mass., 2000).

Thomas G. Paterson, *On Every Front: The Making and Unmaking of the Cold War* (New York, 1992).

Christopher Thorne, *The Issue of War: States, Societies, and the Far Eastern Conflict of 1941–1945* (New York, 1985).

Dimitri Volkogonov, *Stalin* (New York, 1991).

Chapter 2

Carolyn Eisenberg, *Drawing the Line: The American Decision to Divide Germany, 1944–1949* (New York, 1996).

Michael J. Hogan, *The Marshall Plan: America, Britain, and the Reconstruction of Western Europe, 1947–1952* (New York, 1987).

Melvyn P. Leffler, *A Preponderance of Power: National Security, the Truman Administration, and the Cold War* (Stanford, Calif., 1992).

Eduard Mark, 'Revolution by Degrees: Stalin's National-Front Strategy for Europe, 1941–1947', Cold War International History Project Working Paper #31 (2001).

Arnold Offner, *Another Such Victory: President Truman and the Cold War, 1945–1953* (Stanford, Calif., 2002).

Marc Trachtenberg, *A Constructed Peace: The Making of the European Settlement, 1945–1963* (Princeton, 1999).

Daniel Yergin, *Shattered Peace: The Origins of the Cold War and the National Security State* (Boston, 1978).

Chapter 3

William S. Borden, *The Pacific Alliance: United States Foreign Economic Policy and Japanese Trade Recovery, 1947–1955* (Madison, Wis., 1984).

Bruce Cumings, *The Origins of the Korean War* (2 vols, Princeton, 1981 and 1990).

John W. Dower, *Embracing Defeat: Japan in the Wake of World War II* (New York, 1999).

Sergei N. Goncharov, John W. Lewis, and Xue Litai, *Uncertain Partners: Stalin, Mao, and the Korean War* (Stanford, Calif., 1993).

Chen Jian, *Mao's China and the Cold War* (Chapel Hill, N.C., 2001).

Robert J. McMahon, *The Limits of Empire: The United States and Southeast Asia since World War II* (New York, 1999).

Michael Schaller, *The American Occupation of Japan: The Origins of the Cold War in Asia* (New York, 1985).

William Stueck, *The Korean War: An International History* (Princeton, 1995).

Chapter 4

Gordon H. Chang, *Friends and Enemies: The United States, China, and the Soviet Union, 1948–1972* (Stanford, Calif., 1990).

Saki Dockrill, *Eisenhower's New Look National Security Policy, 1953–61* (London, 1996).

Steven Z. Freiberger, *Dawn over Suez: The Rise of American Power in the Middle East* (Chicago, 1992).

Richard H. Immerman, *John Foster Dulles* (Wilmington, Del., 1999).

Wm Roger Louis and Roger Owen (eds.), *Suez 1956: The Crisis and Its Consequences* (New York, 1989).

Stephen G. Rabe, *Eisenhower and Latin America* (Chapel Hill, N.C., 1988).

James G. Richter, *Khrushchev's Double Bind* (Baltimore, 1994).

Chapter 5

Lawrence Freedman, *Kennedy's Wars: Berlin, Cuba, Laos, and Vietnam* (New York, 2000).

Aleksandr Fursenko and Timothy Naftali, *'One Hell of a Gamble': Khrushchev, Castro, and Kennedy, 1958–1964* (New York, 1997).

Fredrik Logevall, *Choosing War: The Lost Chance for Peace and the Escalation of the War in Vietnam* (Berkeley, 1999).

Thomas G. Paterson (ed.), *Kennedy's Search for Victory* (New York, 1989).

Qiang Zhai, *China and the Vietnam Wars, 1950–1975* (Chapel Hill, N.C., 2000).

Chapter 6

Thomas Borstelmann, *The Cold War and the Color Line: American Race Relations in the Global Arena* (Cambridge, Mass., 2001).

Peter J. Kuznick and James Gilbert (eds.), *Rethinking Cold War Culture* (Washington, 2001).

Robert J. McMahon, *The Cold War on the Periphery: The United States, India, and Pakistan* (New York, 1994).

David Reynolds, *One World Divisible: A Global History since 1945* (New York, 2000).

Michael S. Sherry, *In the Shadow of War: The United States since the 1930s* (New Haven, Conn., 1995).

Stephen J. Whitfield, *The Culture of the Cold War* (Baltimore, 1991).

John Young, *Cold War Europe, 1945–89: A Political History* (London, 1991).

Chapter 7

Henry Kissinger, *White House Years* (Boston, 1979).

David Reynolds, *One World Divisible: A Global History since 1945* (New York, 2000).

Raymond L. Garthoff, *Detente and Confrontation: American-Soviet Relations from Nixon to Reagan* (Washington, 1985).

H. W. Brands, *Since Vietnam: The United States in World Affairs, 1973–1995* (New York, 1996).

H. W. Brands, *The Devil We Knew: Americans and the Cold War* (New York, 1993).

John Lewis Gaddis, *Strategies of Containment: A Critical Appraisal of Postwar American National Security Policy* (New York, 1982).

Odd Arne Westad (ed.), *The Fall of Detente: Soviet-American Relations during the Carter Years* (Oslo, 1997).

Gaddis Smith, *Morality, Reason, and Power: American Diplomacy in the Carter Years* (New York, 1986).

Walter LaFeber, *America, Russia, and the Cold War, 1945–2000*, 9th
edn. (New York, 2000).

Chapter 8

David Cortright, *Peace Works: The Citizen's Role in Ending the Cold
War* (Boulder, Co., 1993).

Robert D. English, *Russia and the Idea of the West: Gorbachev,
Intellectuals, and the End of the Cold War* (New York, 2000).

Matthew Evangelista, *Unarmed Forces: The Transnational Movement
to End the Cold War* (Ithaca, New York, 1999).

Raymond L. Garthoff, *The Great Transition: American-Soviet Relations
and the End of the Cold War* (Washington, 1994).

Michael J. Hogan (ed.), *The End of the Cold War: Its Meaning and
Implications* (New York, 1992).

Jacques Levesque, *The Enigma of 1989: The USSR and the Liberation of
Eastern Europe* (Berkeley, 1987).

Olav Njolstad, *The Cold War in the 1980's* (London, forthcoming).

Don Oberdorfer, *The Turn: From the Cold War to a New Era* (New York,
1992).

George P. Shultz, *Turmoil and Triumph: My Years as Secretary of State*
(New York, 1993).

Philip Zelikow and Condoleeza Rice, *Germany Unified and Europe
Transformed: A Study in Statecraft* (Cambridge, Mass., 1995).

Index

Globalization

Visit the
VERY SHORT
INTRODUCTIONS
Web site

www.oup.co.uk/vsi

➤ **Information** about all published titles

➤ News of **forthcoming books**

➤ **Extracts** from the books, including titles
   not yet published

➤ **Reviews** and views

➤ **Links** to other **web sites** and main
   OUP web page

➤ Information about **VSIs in translation**

➤ **Contact** the editors

➤ **Order** other **VSIs** on-line